eric
parry architects

e
pa

volume 5

Introduction: Detailing Topography
David Leatherbarrow

Peripety is the shift of action towards the opposite pole.
Aristotle, *Poetics*

The complete transmutation ... will make itself known naturally every time the conditions are rendered favorable by the given facts: the coupling of two realities, irreconcilable in appearance, upon a plane which apparently does not suit them.
Max Ernst, *Beyond Painting*

[In Freud's study] the resonances continued in abundance, with the cabinet of winged figures and that of vessels and containers flanking the door to his book-lined study, and his writing table, at which the sequence found a culminating reflective intensity, lightened by the enigmatic smile of the figure of a Chinese scholar whom Freud is said to have greeted each day when he came into his study.
Eric Parry, *Context*

Urban topography, vividly evident in the work this volume presents, can be characterised as a mosaic structure of social and spatial conditions, each of which would seem unrelated when thought about individually: a town hall backing onto a cemetery, for example, or a workshop beneath a clinic, or gallery alongside a garage.[1] Conjunctions like these, on city streets and squares, in your city or mine, are rather like the coupling of irreconcilables to which Max Ernst refers: surprising when encountered – surprisingly delightful – and productive, in the ways that word combinations in metaphor augment conventional understanding – a laughing meadow. Differences are continually discovered in terrain that's typically urban, contrast and complementarity structure relationships between institutions or situations that one would have thought were distinct. Behind my house in Philadelphia a tram station, cemetery entrance and row of houses share the same small square, not to the detriment, instead the enrichment of one another. Sometimes adjacencies like this seem unreconciled and incompatible, in the sense that Ernst intended, though he was writing in praise of surrealist objects. But urban architecture seeks to make the discordant seem concordant, at least for a while, thanks to the peripety Aristotle said was characteristic of compelling drama. Much of Eric Parry's architecture is structured similarly, presenting unlikely combinations that are at once dramatic and essentially urban.

Contrasting sharply with this approach and thought, modernist theory presented space as an all-embracing framework architectural expression, an unlimited container for all possible contents, uniform throughout, always yielding, and consistent in itself.

1   The brief comments about the nature of urban topography that follow restate in abbreviated terms fuller explanations set out in David Leatherbarrow, "Introduction: The Topographical Premises of Architecture and Landscape Architecture", *Topographical Stories* (Philadelphia: University of Pennsylvania Press, 2004), pp. 1–16.

The fact that space so conceived never existed or exists in any given site – it is essentially a conceptual representation of locations – did not prevent it from being used as a framework for design in the modern period. Even though modernist urbanism is a project few today are willing to endorse, these days we still speak of space as something that flows, rendered palpable most vividly in circulation networks, where ease of access and passage is prized above all else.

Urban topography is just the opposite of space thought about in this way, it is not mono- but polytropic, not homo- but heterogenous, and not conceptual but concrete, for its regions contrast, conflict and sometimes, through good design, converse with one another. Yet it is not a field of infinite difference either. Topography continually offers experience both unexpected and familiar situations, but not instantly. If space advances its array all at once (in simultaneity), topography gives its locations in time. In any given site, at any given moment, its structure requires that some places be recalled, others anticipated. For this reason, urban topography articulates cultural history and measures human finitude.

How might contemporary design contribute to, or participate in, urban topography understood in this way? In short, through all manner of *reversals*, in the sense of peripety – dramatic change of fortune – defined above. Considering the buildings and projects shown in this volume, one can see a number of plot-making tactics at play. For the sake of brevity, I'll exemplify five in these introductory comments:

re-positioning,
re-typing,
re-centring,
re-grounding, and
re-locating.

My hope is that this account of design operations and representative examples will introduce the artistic and intellectual richness one finds in this book. Because the buildings are presented so clearly and fully in the chapters that follow, I'll focus on a few details that can be used as keys to the methods and configurations that discover in our world of disconnected episodes and incidents a surprising degree of coherence that was prior to these projects latent. Freud, to whom Parry referred in his book called *Context*, explained that psychoanalysis "is accustomed to divine secret and concealed things from [typically] unconsidered and unnoticed details". I'll proceed similarly, with an eye for the ways Parry details urban topography.

Re-positioning

As above, so below, a familiar commonplace of pre-modern thought, governed much of the creative work in architecture in centuries before our own, as it did work in the other topographical arts, landscape architecture and urbanism. Celestial patterns, together with their geometric representation, were often interpreted as models for terrestrial configurations, of sacred sites especially.[2] But in modern work, in its most strident manifestations particularly, the terms were provocatively reversed, the world was 'turned upside down'. Indicative historical precedents for this manner of 'revolution' were the seventeenth-century English Reformation campaigns, when a popular song had this very phrase as its title, perhaps also a musical trope.[3] But maybe the hierarchy that seems so obvious, serene sky setting the rules for unsettled soil, isn't so obvious after all, given the many instances of domes in grottos and gardens on roofs.

Designing a site plan normally requires direct engagement with a site's circumstantial contingencies, irregular though they may be: non-parallelism of nearby streets and their buildings, undesired slopes from one side to another, or unwelcome proximities and distances. The problem isn't new to cities, maybe it's normal in urban architecture. But it needn't be defeating. In the illustrations of his early seventeenth-century treatise, Vincenzo Scamozzi found room for a perfectly square courtyard at the centre of an urban site by adjusting the proportions and shapes of the rooms at his building's edges, a procedure he called "redeeming an irregular site."[4] A baroque case, more elaborate at its centre, would be Antoine Le Pautre's Hôtel de Beauvais in Paris. The ground plan of Eric Parry's Fen Court does something very similar, though his interpretation is more surprising. What's more, the displacement or re-positioning of geometries typically found above to below is just half the building's story, for there exists on the roof a similarly topsy-turvy conjunction, though the upper deck's perimeter orients experience and knowledge much more widely than its street-level analogue.

2   Of the many ancient sources that have been proposed as its origin, lines from the *Emerald Tablet* of Hermes Trismegistus elaborate the notion rather clearly: "That which is below corresponds to that which is above."
3   An authoritative and colourful account is given in Christopher Hill, *The World Turned Upside Down. Radical Ideas During the English Revolution* (London, 1977). Again, the origin of the phrase is ancient, but this time Biblical: "But the other Jews which believed not, moved with envy, took unto them certain lewd fellows of the baser sort, and gathered a company, and set all the city on an uproar, and assaulted the house of Jason, and sought to bring them out to the people. And when they found them not, they drew Jason and certain brethren unto the rulers of the city, crying, 'These that have turned the world upside down are come hither also'". *Acts* 17: 5–6
4   Scamozzi, *L'Idea dell Architettura Universale* [1615] (1982), Bk. 3, Ch. 10, pp. 256–62.

Pencil and crayon drawing by Eric Parry and David Dernie, dating from 1985, depicting Victor Horta's Hôtel Tassel in Brussels. The section through the lightwell and stair is accompanied by the canted plan of the entrance.

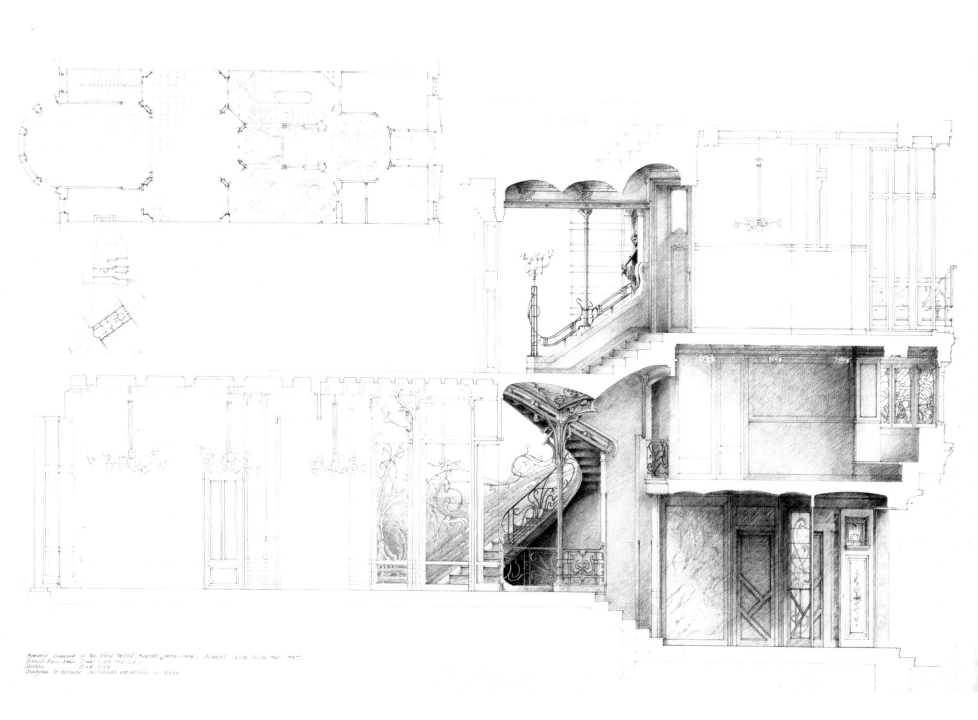

Measured drawing of the Hotel Tassel, Brussels (1892-1893), Architect: Victor Horta (1861-1947)
Ground Floor Plan   Scale 1:100 (here 1:8)
Section   Scale 1:100
Diagram to describe sectional projection 1:1000

Regular geometries that correspond to sky patterns and irregular forms that indicate variations in terrain are compressed together in Fen Court's site and roof plans – a square plus a meandering edge centring pedestrian paths, and cubic volumes within a trellis on the roof. The ground-level courtyard's square ceiling presents an unexpected and delightful video image of the surrounding urban landscape, while the roof plane concentrates arrival and departure in a green glass block that middles both the plan's varied perimeter and the outward spread of the raised lattice. Thus, the building's vertical limits re-position conditions that are ostensibly above and below. But these improbable conjunctions do more than delight. *Disorientation acts as a prelude to re-orientation.* At Fen Court preliminary engagement with the building's immediate vicinity is followed by outward reach. Upside-down or down-side up, the worlds in and outside the building are shown to behave as one.

Re-typing

The notion of type is a key topic in Aldo Rossi's arguments about the architecture of the city. It is not only the "analytical moment" in architecture, through which some measure of rationality in urban understanding can be achieved, but is also an instrument of project development, as was subsequently implied (a year after Rossi's book) by Alan Colquhoun in his account of typology as a design method. Types persist, while "models" succeed one another in time. Monuments render architecture's staying power legible. Should we conclude from Rossi and Colquhoun that types don't change, even though buildings do?

Eric Parry's project on Seymour Street suggests maybe they do or can. The case in point is in London's terrace house type. In *Georgian London*, Sir John Summerson famously and beautifully explained its key elements, also its ubiquity throughout the city, and its surprisingly different manifestations when built (differences of width, depth and apertures), as well as construction materials and techniques. Still, through all the variation, there was the type's "idiomatic" verticality, Summerson observed, also its raised level (the *terrace*) at the front, lower mews behind, masked party walls along the façade's running length, serial repetition of windows and doors, and so on. It would seem this type has indeed persisted without change from the late seventeenth century to our time. Yet, there have also been many interpretations that broke the rules, without rendering the innovation senseless: the Adelphi Terrace by the Adam brothers, for example, or the three houses that Soane joined together to make his house/ museum. Eric Parry's project should be classed in this latter group

– types that re-type. Might work of this kind indicate how continuity in urban architecture and culture can be achieved *through*, not *despite* change?

As with the masking of structure in traditional interpretations of the terrace-house type, the row of 'houses' on Seymour Street appears to be one. It is not only this façade's continuous planarity that supports the one-house reading, several elements that incessantly repeat do likewise: the two-window balconies, the single-window cornice cut-outs, the very thin sills, and so on. Entries to Georgian terrace houses are generally set above the sidewalk level by one or a few steps and are almost universally a-symmetrical within the façade composition. Although there aren't any entry steps at Seymour Street, its base does position the threshold off to the side of the façade's centre line, and against the grain of the balconies and cornice glazings that run from edge to edge. It also extends that break vertically, with giant white pilasters, whose vertical reach stops short of the top edge of the window frames they adjoin. The detail that strikes one most, however, is the termination of each intermediate pilaster in its corresponding balcony, cutting it off before it meets the ground. I believe the element's a-typicality attests to the façade's several tasks: 1) making one house out of many, 2) marking the building's main entry, and 3) providing a permeable base for the building's public functions.

The a-typicalites of this building are these: many houses as one, fronted by a wall-with-windows that has at its base windows-as-a-wall, each of which is sheltered by repetitive elements whose pattern is interrupted by a gate-like imposition that is made up of uncapped pilasters that are alternately grounded and baseless, standing in front of a frame structure that allows itself to be read as wall construction. Types that are re-typed in these ways allow a richness of reading and density of content that allegiance to norms would surely have made more difficult, if not prevented.

Re-centring

Gottfried Semper, in his unfinished *Theory of Formal Beauty*, differentiated three structural dimensions of a body or building's formal beauty: 1) symmetry, which he called its macrocosmic unit of order, 2) proportionality, its microcosmic unit of order, and 3) direction. He noted in passing that these three correspond to the three spatial directions. Still more interesting, and somewhat surprising, is his fourth centre of relations, the cardinal point of the phenomenon, *its purpose*, a higher order, he said, that can culminate in character and expression. The incomplete and somewhat murky quality of the text has given rise to much debate about his meaning, particularly the externality or immanent character of "purpose". And though he hurried on to other aspects of formal beauty in his lecture, never really elaborating his understanding of a phenomenon's "cardinal point," Semper seems to have suggested that the principle of fitness to purpose would allow re-arrangement of customary relationships between symmetries, proportions and directions. Such is the case, I think, in Parry's project for Buckingham Palace Road.

The project transforms a pre-existing five-bay façade, the former street-side entry to the Parcel Office for Victoria Railway Station. Revolving doors in the glass-walled central three bays admit entrance on foot; the bay to the right, handicap access. The piers and low-slung arch of this bay, too, surround a window-wall, but one that is interestingly elaborate in its sub-divisions – the detail that originally caught my eye. The door-capping horizontal aligns with the analogous elements on the three central entries, though there they bisect circles in plan, while here, on the far right, the geometry of a single-plane door. That door also gets vertical stiffeners on either side, which terminate in the arch above. This pattern is repeated on the far left, without the door that made them necessary. The pairing of the two end bays is also strengthened by one more horizontal, that gives upper and lower parts proportions that are roughly commensurate with the other bits of glazing.

Thus composed, the stone façade's five-bay symmetry and proportionality are preserved, even amplified. But the extra glazing bars on the left still need explanation. For visitors on foot, the axes of configuration perfectly align with axes of movement (in Semper's terms), three bays and three doors, beautifully symmetrical. Entry to the far right, however, has no equivalent on the far left, just as there is only one ramp inside the lobby, pinned to the right-side wall. Also tipping the scales to the right are the hand rails that guide movement up a small section of the wide, side-to-side steps, which, in turn, arrive at the same point of the ramp, in line with the reception desk, and finally, the start of the escalators that rise along the back wall, in the full depth of the space. Hence, the key misalignment, or re-centring: from an even-handed pre-existing front, through a right-leaning plane of glass (within the depth of the massive wall) into a widely lateral hall, fronting the steps and ramp, that re-directs approach off axis, along angles that vary depending on which doorway admitted entry.

Why the re-centring? What Semper called fitness to purpose seems to have been decisive. A prejudice in favour of pre-existing conditions might suggest that re-use in this case – the subtle a-symmetries –

should be deemed mis-use. My sense of it is different. Compressed into the glass and glazing bars of the already-given stone wall are distinct but equally important axes of movement and orientation, intimating configurations in depth before the space is entered. Getting ahead of itself, the space confers orientation. The reversals that result from re-centring are complemented by exchanges in less-tangible qualities: deeper space is made brighter than it typically would be, central space extends vertically (yielding a light-weight work of art), and foreground space manages a transition from axial to diagonal passage, anticipating the dynamism of diagonal movement up the escalators in the distance, itself a sharp contrast with the durable fixity of the entry wall. Likewise, for the design's palpable qualities: thick to thin, black to white, and stone to steel. None of this strikes me as capricious: re-centrings, reversals and substitutions are architectonic means accomplishing practical purposes – architecture's 'cardinal point' – as they unfold in historical and urban circumstances that are no longer used the way they once were.

Re-grounding

Sir John Soane, among other architects active in the late eighteenth and early nineteenth centuries, designed buildings whose lower parts or elements were either eliminated or submerged into the substructure, the soil or streets of their sites. Recall, for example, the powerful but baseless columns he designed for the Bank of England. Projects by figures like F. Weinbrenner, F. Gilly, L. von Klenze, K. F. Schinkel, C. F. Hansen, E. L. Boullée, C. N. Ledoux, or the painted architecture of H. Robert (whose semi-sunken pyramids settle themselves into their sites no less securely than Boullée's cenotaphs), seem to have intended an architecture that is not only inseparable from its ground plane, but partly covered by it. Darkly magnetic earthwork held superimposed frameworks in its grip. Tuscan or Greek (not Roman) Doric became the preferred classical Order (no plinth, torus, scotia or filet), temples were deprived of their crepidoma, or base platforms (stereobate certainly, possibly stylobate also – often connected at the successive set backs with reveal joints), and rusticated wall surfaces from bottom to top. One is at pains to determine if this embedded architecture resulted from the build-up of the surrounding substrate (soil or street), or the settling of the work into softer surfaces – rather like buildings in today's Rome in the first case or Mexico City in the second. To some degree, eighteenth-century architecture's assimilation of the noble into the pedestrian level was anticipated by contemporary garden *fabriques* and architectural ruins. But nature's assertion of its rightful claim on materials taken from its reserves cannot explain the very squat columns, low-slung arches and rustic

walling that typify this un-heeled or shoeless architecture. Solid and secure – much more so than the politics of the time – the buildings are also heavy, in both senses: weighty and burdened.

The installations Parry designed for the exhibition of his drawings and notebooks at Sir John Soane's Museum are just the opposite: lightweight, hovering and un-grounded. Soane's surfaces spread themselves out laterally, joining others, constructing a work that is both aggregate and all-of-a-piece. Parry, by contrast, floats the horizontals, withdrawing their supports from the corners, in order for them to stand on their own (while acknowledging the setting's axiality and double symmetries). A single detail exemplifies Parry's practice of de-basing elements, the negative joint or reveal beneath the plinth of each display case or pedestal, made up of shadow not substance, resisting rather than submitting to gravity's eternal pull, and recessed. The unevenness of the floor made the 1 cm suspension of the plinths on levelling screw pads a sensible, discreet solution. With the shadow-slot in mind, should one say the architecture of the exhibition is out-of-context, because it doesn't conform to the local manner, or does the work's distinct stance allow us to see even more clearly the character of Soane's architecture, in comparison with what it is not?

Though a dialogue between distinct points of view – his and Soane's – seems to have been on Parry's mind, the light-weight levels, together with the stacking and spreading, accommodate the visitor's posture and desire for study with great care and intelligence. Maybe the desire for a gracious and inviting architecture subordinated the professional or disciplinary concern with re-grounding. Short as their stay in the rooms was to be, the works on show were placed in plan and section to be no less accommodating than the furnishings of the house. That thought suggests a gentle critique of Soane: maybe the Museum's aesthetic richness comes at the cost of concerns that the exhibition design shows to be primary in all good architecture.

Re-locating

When John Hejduk explained the pedagogical ambition of the famous Nine Square Problem, used to introduce decades of Cooper Union architecture students to the discipline, he said that it allowed the beginner to grasp the basic elements of architecture: grid, frame, post, beam ... field, edge ... extension, compression ... and so on. Although a sense of fabrication was to be revealed through the study, the educational core of the problem was the set of elements, the rudimentary parts of all architecture. Unlike *fragments*, whose completion can always only be imagined or projected, *elements* assume or require interrelationships that bind them together in an intelligible

whole, though variations within that whole are always allowed. Autonomy is a key characteristic of any configuration governed by regular or lawful interrelationships. It is also a source of intellectual pleasure, a welcome sense that the design has reached an end, even if construction hasn't started, because nothing can be added or taken away, as Alberti famously said of works that are beautiful (intellectually and visually settled). Parry's 1 Undershaft has at its core a nine-square grid. But the work as a whole is far from settled in on itself, nor does its *engaged autonomy*, if a contradiction will be allowed, suggest that self-sameness means self-separation. Perhaps the project indicates that architectural autonomy should be considered in two ways, of conception and realisation, which, when seen in concert, allow a work freedom to define itself within the constraints of its circumstances.

At 1 Undershaft circulation slips out of the central square and extends beyond the plot, at and beneath the urban surface. This building, like just about any that takes its stand in a European capital, has no choice but to engage a perimeter that resulted from a series of historical accidents. Had engagement been understood as conformity to pre-existing conditions the result would have been a mess, no less accidental than the context. Instead, several encounters have been established on terms the building defines for itself, less in plan than section, which is to say at not one but several levels: two storeys at street level, then another two below that, with intermediate mezzanine decks, and then, still farther below, levels for parking. Each of the stacked platforms has its own lateral reach, of surprising extent in the sub-surface instances. Constructing a building of this height is no simple task, but equally demanding is the work of managing the encounter between the tower and its base. The problem of structuring the public realm seems to have been on Parry's mind from the start, given the concerns that are vividly evident in the exacting and elegant study models.

But lateral thinking, and the engagements it intends, is not only evident at the building's perimeter, but is also apparent at its centre. Each of the squares in the three-by-three grid is occupied or interpreted in a different way. Sometimes a sub-square is occupied at its centre, other times its edge. It can also be left open. Perhaps the most provocative interpretation is when a square form escapes its ostensible boundary, declaring interest in something external to the basic arrangement. The key instance of this sort of slippage is of vertical circulation taking its place outside the frame, in yet another square figure. Eccentricity such as this shouldn't be seen as a fault in conception, potentially remedied by restoration of internal coherence, but as an evidence of the ethos I described earlier, *engaged autonomy*, the sort of wholeness that makes itself counterpart to its milieu, and therefore, by definition, partial.

Eric Parry Architects, Seymour Street, completed in 2018 for mixed use, brings together commercial and residential spaces, a space for the local community as well as a restaurant. Here, the north façade of 1–9 Seymour Street is only one of the aspects of the building, which crosses the full depth of the urban block.

D MAZE   ALONG THIS RIVER ROAD   SWEEP ALONG THE SO
MED EARTH   I FIND MYSELF IN OTHER BODY   THESE VAST SHOULDERS THE
AND CLAY   MY BRONZE-GREEN BEARD AND FLOWING LOCKS   ABOVE ME RUN THE TI

The Architecture of Eric Parry Architects: The Poetics of Concreteness
Dagmar Motycka Weston

Eric Parry Architects' Chelsea Barracks, a detail of the southwestern façade of 1 Grenadier Gardens (Building 7) completed in 2021 as part of Phase 4 of the larger development.

One of the striking things about the buildings of Eric Parry Architects is how different they all are. There is little by way of a typical repeating form or material palette, much less a recognisable house style. Instead, each building draws its character from the requirements of its brief and the specific place in which it is situated. In his writings and presentations, Parry often evokes the power of *genius loci*.[1] No location, of course, is a blank canvas; each is formed by a unique set of circumstances: orientation, topography, boundaries, proximities, transparencies. Each had generally taken shape over long periods and provides the architect with constraints and opportunities. Most are embedded in dense and complex urban settings with diverse histories, character and cultural memory. While today sometimes highly fragmented, such typical settings remain valuable as repositories of social custom, relationships and decorum. The challenge is to place a new building within such a web of concrete relationships so that it fulfils its purpose but also contributes meaningfully to its setting. This sometimes includes finding an appropriate expression, which would resonate with the traditions of a specific building type or local materiality. A building situated in this way may also play a generative role, pointing the way to fruitful future development. The type of

contextual approach deployed here is not simply to 'blend in' by the superficial mimicry of the physical features of the surrounding buildings. Instead, an understanding of the deeper pre-existing patterns of the site area becomes the basis for an imaginative interpretation and appropriate architectural response.

This approach is also rooted in what might be called a situational understanding of space. This is in contrast to what often seems like the dominant view, which is rooted in late nineteenth-century perspectivism and which sees architectural space as neutral, isotropic and without inherent meaning.[2] A situational spatiality is unconstricted by preconceived geometrical schemata. It is more akin to a lived, corporeal spatiality in that it stems from the conditions of human embodiment, such as live vision and movement. It is rooted in the experiential world: differentiated, bounded and oriented. The relationships between buildings engender meaning and are thus almost as important as the buildings themselves. Situational spatiality forms concrete places as settings for specific events or activities, and looks to surrounding conditions to form connections and relationships

1   Eric Parry, *Context: Architecture and the Genius of Place*, Chichester: Wiley, 2015.

2   See Dagmar Motycka Weston, "Corporeal Spatiality and the Restorative Fragment in Early Twentieth-Century Art and Architecture", in Henriette Steiner, Max Sternberg, eds, *Phenomenologies of the City*, Farnham: Ashgate, 2015, pp. 194–210.

which always contain human significance. Thus distinct places can be created and engaging metaphorical content may arise. Such a conception in contemporary architecture is foreshadowed by the Arts and Crafts Movement, which in its turn adopted certain qualities of the Picturesque and vernacular traditions. Medieval architecture and especially the Gothic were much admired. In "The Nature of Gothic", John Ruskin praised what he called Gothic's "changefulness", a kind of fluidity and specific responsiveness which allowed it, for example, to place a window where one was needed.[3] Arts and Crafts architecture is characterised by a similar kind of malleability and sensitivity to context. This may be seen clearly in many of the houses of Philip Webb, William Lethaby, C. F. A. Voysey or Frank Lloyd Wright. Subverting an inert classical box, their layout is generally asymmetrical and reactive. They are changeful in Ruskinian terms, their design attentive to the orientation of rooms with respect to daylight and views. Existing buildings and topographical elements are sometimes incorporated, forming outdoor settings such as courts or gardens, and strong reciprocities between parts. Instead of an instant visual impact as a complete image, they are to be discovered gradually through movement. Webb's Standen House (incidentally much admired by Parry) exemplifies all of these features.[4]

Le Corbusier was one of the first modernist architects to develop – through his own early grounding in Ruskin and the Arts and Crafts,[5] and through his subsequent work alongside Amédée Ozenfant on Purism – a kind of situational spatiality. This would be manifest in his interwar villas and most of his painting. The theme of the *promenade architecturale*, for example, was based in the embodied inhabitant's moving through and perceiving a sequence of events staged within the implicit spatiality of the buildings. The journey from the ground to the roof terrace, involving climbing, touch and both interior and exterior views, carried thematic content. During the 1920s, this would often entail a transformative progression from an ambiguous chthonic realm of the ground level to a geometric resolution and full light on the roof terrace, where a redemptive communion with nature would take place. The Purist villas are also rich with memorable places conceived as settings for particular scenarios to unfold. The small gallery perched above the ramp and the horizon of the salon windows at the Maison La Roche is one such place. Equipped with built-in book shelves, a warming chimney, a *chaise longue* and a window in the tree tops,

it provides a setting for repose, reading and looking out. In addition, these buildings are often – in marked contrast to Le Corbusier's contemporaneous urbanism – highly responsive to the concrete circumstances of their wider location. As in Purist still life, spatial and thematic relationships between architectural elements, facilitated by a situational spatiality, were key to a Corbusian poetics of dwelling.

In a similar way, Eric Parry Architects values the given conditions and palimpsest-like textures of each of their sites. Parry has repeatedly noted the importance and poetic power of the "rich topography of urban adjacencies", which animates his architecture.[6] And while the situational spatiality of their architecture may owe something to the Arts and Crafts, much of their contextual practice is due to a love and an extensive understanding of cities, many of which Parry came to know in the company of friends and colleagues, such as Dalibor Vesely, Joseph Rykwert and Kenneth Frampton. This understanding involves a recognition of a pre-existing order of the city, of its histories and traditional patterns. The archetypal settings of the street and square, for example, are seen as fundamental building blocks. They are characterised by a hierarchy of the principal and the secondary, of the public and private domains, the kinds of life they generate and the stories they tell. Due to the relative stability of human needs, a sense of decorum is latently present in our urban traditions. It suggests what kind of architectural response is appropriate, for example, in a principal street (more formal, focused on supporting an existing street wall), a minor lane or a garden court (freer, allowing for private life and individual idiosyncrasies). The fact that fragmentation has become almost the norm in many of today's cities does not make these urban traditions irrelevant. A recognition and recovery of such an order enables the city to evolve and change without losing a sense of continuity. Some branches of the Modern Movement, such as Futurism, were keen to explode this principle along with what they saw as other outmoded traditions. Yet, a civic order, arising from an accretion of cultural custom and experience, is essential because it makes the city comprehensible and provides a meaningful alternative to arbitrariness. Legibility is needed if the public realm is to perform its ethical function of allowing citizens to feel at ease in their community and the city. Parry's interest in these enduring urban structures was also manifest in the projects he devised during his 14 years as a lecturer in Architecture at the University of Cambridge, where his students were often asked to study the history and typical forms of some characteristic street or neighbourhood as a starting point for design.

3   John Ruskin, "The Nature of Gothic", in *The Stones of Venice*. Vol II, London: George Allen, 1898.
4   See Sheila Kirk, *Philip Webb: Pioneer of Arts and Crafts Architecture*, Chichester: Wiley, 2005, pp. 150–60.
5   See Mary Patricia May Sekler "Le Corbusier, Ruskin, the Tree and the Open Hand", in *The Open Hand Essays on Le Corbusier*, Cambridge Mass.: MIT Press, 1982, pp. 42–95.
6   See Eric Parry "Juxtaposing the New and the Old", *Architectural Design*, January 2016, Vol. 86 (1), p. 36.

The landing at the top of the ramp of Le Corbusier and Pierre Jeanneret's Maison La Roche, in Paris, 1923–25, home to the Foundation Le Corbusier.

Most architects follow these principles to some extent, and the frequent references in current architectural discourse to 'placemaking' would seem to confirm this. However, for Eric Parry Architects, an openness to the richness of a given context, its history and its varying meaning, has become a design strategy and a source of architectural invention. Parry agrees with his late friend and colleague Dalibor Vesely, who had argued that "to avoid the meaninglessness of the contemporary city it [...] is possible to start from the given reality of any existing city and to discover [...] a residuum of tradition sufficient to support a consistent imaginative and sometimes even radical reinterpretation of the status quo."[7] Such an emphasis on the generative qualities of the historical and physical context is evident, for example, at Eric Parry Architects' Leathersellers' Seventh Hall in the City of London.[8]

The projects in the present volume illustrate a situational sensibility working at a range of scales. It is evident in miniature in the interventions Parry made for an exhibition of his drawings within the rich fabric of Sir John Soane's Museum, where each new display cabinet took its form and meanings from the setting in which it was placed. At the medium scale of the house, the Lipton residence may be seen as an architectural dialogue – embodied in one coherent structure – between the decorum of a restrained classicising façade and the atavistic freedoms of the private world of back terraces and gardens. At the urban scale, a highly contextual approach is evident in the planning of the Fen Court office building, where each side creates meaningful ground-level connections and transparencies with the adjacent streets and memorial garden.[9]

The Civic Façade

An important aspect of the situational approach is the treatment of the architectural façade. As the communicative face of the building, which in some ways echoes the directionality of the human body, the façade has traditionally been a thick, representational layer mediating between the building interior and its surroundings. Equally important has been its role as a scenographic background to the varied theatre of urban life, and in providing essential legibility to the

7   Dalibor Vesely, *Architecture and Continuity*, Themes Series, London: Architectural Association, 1982, p. 12, quoted by Eric Parry, "Juxtaposing the New and the Old", p. 35.
8   See Eric Parry, "Architect's View", *The Leathersellers' Review 2015/2016*, pp. 14–15 and Dagmar Motycka Weston, *The Seventh Hall of the Leathersellers' Company*, London: Artifice Press, 2020.
9   See chapters on Sir John Soane's Museum, pp. 132–43, Lipton Residence II, pp. 144–57, and Fen Court. pp. 26–39 in the present volume.

city. The composed planar, hierarchical façade generally fell out of favour with the architects of the Modern Movement, who tended to see it as upholding outdated hierarchies and hiding all manner of ills. In his urbanist polemics, Le Corbusier, for example, saw the façade as belonging to the despised "canyon street" and as putting a presentable mask on the insalubrious world of back lanes and courts of "tubercular Paris" beyond.[10] He sought to liberate the façade from such tasks by his Five Points for a New Architecture. The design of many modernist housing estates concentrated on the blocks' interiors as receptacles of fresh air and sunshine rather than on their outward appearance. Parallel to this, there was sometimes a focus on the building as an independent sculptural object in the round, with all sides having equal compositional significance. Gerrit Rietveld's Schröder House, with its De Stijl composition of solids and voids, of concrete and glass planes, and designed in almost entirely abstract space, is perhaps the most complete example of this tendency.[11] The modernist preoccupation with the ethical implications of glass and transparency, and a resulting preference for large expanses of glazing, also contributed strongly to the dissolution of the communicative façade. The glass curtain wall, often degraded by the exigencies of commercial development, came to dominate the urban landscape. The prevailing idea, memorably summed up in a seminal modernist manifesto, was that a building's exterior should be – "like a soap bubble" – a direct expression of the interior.[12] This also signalled a rejection of the traditional façade. And yet, the differentiated, oriented and representational façade has an essential role to play in providing human scale and elucidating the civic order.

This is perhaps one of the reasons why the work of Eric Parry Architects generally embraces many of the traditional civic responsibilities of the architectural façade but interprets them in new ways. Parry sees architecture and the urban public realm as having deep connections with scenography, understood in its broadest sense as the festive setting for the performance of civic activities and social engagement.[13] Among many built examples, the montage of retained and new façades which encloses the One Eagle Place development – ranging from the most festive and eye-catching on Piccadilly to the more restrained in the quiet side lane – perhaps stands out.[14] In the buildings comprising the present volume, one is struck by how differing context conditions inform the design of the projects' elevations and consequently also the arrangements of the interior. The practice's relaxation with respect to the "soap bubble" principle speaks of the prioritisation of a coherent urban order over the outward expression of the private domain. This can be seen, for example, in Vicarage Gate House, where the formal front façade is designed to echo and complement those of the surrounding historical terraces.[15]

Poetic Making and the Material Imagination

Eric Parry Architects belongs to a select group of contemporary practices characterised by a high degree of commitment to the tectonic and material qualities of their projects, their preoccupation pre-dating the current burst of interest in the subject. It determines which materials are selected and how components are fabricated, detailed and assembled, so as to bring out their inherent physical and thematic qualities. For some time, the emphasis in some branches of the architectural profession has been on novel 'iconic' forms, where buildings are mainly consumed on the level of the disembodied, visual image. By contrast, the practice's work shows an understanding that the rich physicality of architecture – its tectonic and corporeal dimensions, made manifest in a high quality of execution – is a basic prerequisite of its success. The architects often emphasise the sensory experience of their buildings: the haptic pleasure of a well-made wooden handrail, the scent of leather upholstery, the acoustic intimacy of a wood or horsehair-panelled interior. Their design is usually an exploration of ways in which superb craftsmanship and detailing can be married to modern industrial manufacture and construction methods. The physical reality of things is celebrated for its utility and beauty, and as a way of provoking the imagination. These preoccupations are again evident in Parry's writings, where a genuine enthusiasm for materials – their essential qualities and the appropriate manner of their handling in specific circumstances – is palpable. For him, good architecture must always have a tectonic resonance.

These principles can be traced to the architect's background experiences. Throughout his career Parry has retained a love of hand drawing as an essential part of the creative process.[16] As a student, he had a short

10   Le Corbusier, *The Radiant City*, London: Faber & Faber, 1967, p. 91.
11   It is no accident that period photos rarely showed the house in its earth-bound existing context, as an end to a traditional residential terrace.
12   Le Corbusier, *Towards a New Architecture* (1923), London: Architectural Press, 1970. Le Corbusier himself rarely fully adhered to this dictum, designing some highly contextual urban façades, as at the 1928 Maison Planeix in Paris.
13   See Christian Frost, "Interview with Eric Parry", *Architecture and Culture*, 6:3, 2018, pp. 505–17.
14   See Jay Merrick, *Eric Parry Architects Vol 4*, London: Artifice Press, 2018, pp. 42–55.
15   See chapter on Vicarage Gate House in the present volume, pp. 110–21.
16   See *Eric Parry Drawing*, London: Sir John Soane's Museum, 2019.

Detail of the wisteria on Fen
Court's roof garden in May 2023.

but formative stint at the office of the architect John Brandon-Jones, a noted historian of the Arts and Crafts Movement in architecture and a one-time professional partner of C. F. A. Voysey. Brandon-Jones promoted continuity with the past and traditional techniques, such as the making of measured drawings, at a time when these ideas were seen as irrelevant or even subversive by hard-core modernists. The office held an archive of Philip Webb drawings, which Parry studied and admired, and this stimulated a deep interest in the Arts and Crafts approach to materials and making, and to the integration of architecture and the applied arts. Similar concerns informed his graduate studies at the Royal College of Art, a design school which brought together a range of art and craft disciplines, promoting the unity of design and fabrication, of the studio and the workshop. There he also became acquainted with many artists, for whom the production of their work was a very hands-on activity. These interests would be explored during his time in academia. While at Cambridge, Parry devised a course on the iconography of materials, which looked at their inherent qualities and meaning in a cultural context. During this time, he also explored themes of what has since become known as 'material imagination', as for example it appears in the architecture of the Bavarian Rococo or Belgian Art Nouveau. Similar ideas had also inspired certain strands of Surrealism, which celebrated the concreteness and metaphoricity of the phenomenal world, a philosophical approach popularised in architectural education primarily by Dalibor Vesely. Subsequently these themes would be among those informing Parry's architectural practice. He served on advisory committees for several key historic buildings and was elected Royal Academician in 2006. The possibilities of fruitful interaction between architectural design, making and the arts continue to preoccupy him.

The ideas of the Arts and Crafts Movement, stripped of the hesitancy toward modern technology, continue to cast a long shadow over some of the more interesting domains of today's architectural practice. For the artists and architects of this movement, good craftsmanship and the integrity of fine materials, deployed in straight-forward but expressive ways, became ethical principles. Their artefacts were to replace the degraded, overly ornate output of industrial production, which had become the norm during the nineteenth century, helping also to restore the dignity of work. The movement promoted the integration of architecture and the applied arts, reviving traditional crafts. It provided an important early impetus to similar design movements on the Continent, such as the Deutscher Werkbund and the Bauhaus. The latter has been particularly significant for the development of twentieth-century architecture in showing how

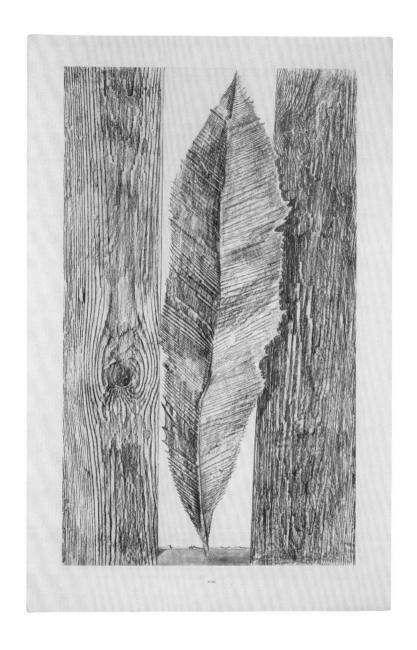

Max Ernst, *Les Mœurs des feuilles* (c.1925) in his *Histoire naturelle* (Galerie Jeanne Bucher: Paris, 1926).

good contemporary design may be achieved and made affordable through the creative use of the new industrial materials and machine production. Certain practitioners of the Modern Movement – notably Mies van der Rohe and Adolf Loos, each coming from a crafting background – would create an architecture in which sumptuous and elegantly detailed materials, such as bronze, exotic stones and fine woods, could provide continuity with the past and bring a luxurious tactility and thematic content to their buildings. Eric Parry Architects' praxis can perhaps be situated somewhere in this tradition. They too have an active interest in traditional crafts, such as textile design, tapestry making, bronze casting and leatherworking, and incorporate them into their entirely contemporary tectonic language. In a way reminiscent of their early modernist predecessors, they push back against the shallow norms of today's globalised commercial architectural production. Their efforts also have an ethical grounding.

There are many examples of outstanding making in the work of the current volume, where a range of materials is used imaginatively and where tectonic traditions are often appreciated for their typicality and cultural context. Parry speaks with enthusiasm of the old French technique of zinc sheeting manufacture, for example, which came to supply virtually all the characteristic mansard roofs and dormers of Second Empire Paris, the blue-grey roofscape becoming a familiar feature of Impressionist painting.[17] His fascination with craft and making is perhaps most conspicuous in the practice's extensive work with glazed ceramics, a craft developed to its peak by English Arts and Crafts potteries during the Industrial Revolution. He sees the making of ceramics as a mysterious, artificial and almost alchemical process.

Parry's ethos of combining contemporary design with traditional crafting may be seen in microcosm in the pieces of furniture created as part of certain projects.[18] The Vigilia bench was originally designed to complement the serenity of the Dick Sheppard Chapel at St Martin-in-the-Fields. It combines delicate, hand-turned oak spindles of the backrest and legs with the robust, subtly contoured oak seat and back rail. The bench is made by traditional joinery techniques and recalls some Arts and Crafts furniture, such as William Morris's popular Suffolk chair range. The traditional feel is, however, subverted by the contemporary steel cross bracing and by the bent metal junction plates which anchor it and the legs to the seat. These elements celebrate tectonic necessities by turning them into

ornamental motifs. Referencing similar cross bracing of the iconic Eames bucket chair, the bench embodies a reciprocity between traditional crafting and the modern spirit. The seat is upholstered in a durable and beautiful horsehair textile of a natural brown-grey colour. This material, a frequent element in the practice's interiors, is the product of an ancient and now very rare craft, deployed in a contemporary manner.

A similar story is told in the work by other tectonic techniques. In contrast to the thin-veneer qualities of some contemporary cladding, Eric Parry Architects generally deploys exterior materials attached to the structural frame as a thick and substantial layer. This not only resonates with a particular place, but also ensures robustness and durability. Façades clad in stone, brick or ceramic are detailed with deep reveals and recessed or projecting features to recreate the massiveness and rich shadow play of traditional masonry construction. Interesting instances of the use of brick or stone cladding as a heavy, sensual material are to be found at Vicarage Gate House, 111 Buckingham Palace Road and Chelsea Barracks' Phase 4.[19] The practice was an early proponent of the recent revival of interest in the structural use of stone, which had been facilitated by modern quarrying and cutting methods. Stone has since been recognised as one of the more eco-friendly building materials.

Eric Parry Architects also often deploys ceramic cladding, either as a rain screen or traditionally hand-set with lime mortar. Parry likes the versatility of ceramic, which can be used as individually cast forms or as the more economical die-extruded sections. Most importantly, the material's durable finish has the ability to create dramatic, changeable effects of light and colour. His occasional discussions of the experimentation which had gone into finding just the right range of ceramic glaze qualities for use in a particular project reveal a deep commitment and considerable technical knowledge.[20] The use of projecting vertical ribs on some of the buildings helps control solar gain while also lending a spatial ambiguity to the façades, making them appear transparent when seen head on, but variably veiled when viewed obliquely from the streets below. This effect animates the façades of Fen Court and One Chamberlain Square.[21] The practice also sometimes design highly crafted, bespoke metal elements. These are expressive of the tectonic nature of the material in its structural strength or its metamorphic potential in casting. The striking

17   Eric Parry, *Context*, pp. 133–35.
18   See Edwin Heathcote, *Eric Parry Architects Vol 3*, Artifice Press: London, 2016, pp. 181–92.

19   See chapters on Vicarage Gate House, pp. 110–21, 111 Buckingham Palace Road, pp. 122–31, and Chelsea Barracks, pp. 172–93 in the present volume.
20   See Eric Parry, *Context*, pp. 167–68.
21   See chapters on Fen Court, pp. 26–39 and One Chamberlain Square, pp. 80–95 in the present volume.

structure, accentuated joint details and engaging material qualities of these sculptural set pieces become an ornamental motif. At Carlton House Terrace, the wintergarden atrium, which is the luminous centre of the building, contains two such pieces: the apparently floating steel-plate staircase and the cascading wrought-iron planter suspended through three levels.[22]

Some of the most lyrical moments in the practice's work seem to draw on the afore-mentioned theme of material imagination. Rooted in a phenomenological understanding, and first propounded by the philosopher of matter Gaston Bachelard, material imagination is part of an attempt to restore a reciprocity between a rationalist, instrumental definition of materials and a more primary, situated understanding, which had informed pre-modern and craft culture, and which remains latently available to us through our experience of the world. It implies an exploration of the ways in which the concrete elements of daily life partake of analogy, draw on cultural archetypes and intertwine with memory and daydream. It is a remarkable characteristic of human perception that things in the experiential world are never isolated 'objects' but are situated in a web of tacit connections. The phenomenon of the imagination 'throwing a bridge' of analogy between apparently unrelated things was understood by the Surrealists as the origin of the poetic image. The spark engendered by such incongruous juxtapositions was the basis of the marvellous in their poetry and art, especially collage.[23] In such works of automatism as the *frottages* of Max Ernst, for example, the found elements of daily reality were transformed when wedded to other things. A wood grain texture, untethered from its customary setting and scale, metamorphosed into a feather, leaf or tree, adding to the hallucinatory atmosphere of the image.[24] Such latent correspondences between things in the world poetically highlight the richness and mystery of existence. In architecture, a similar theme may be found when one material is used deliberately to call to mind another, thus subverting the rigid, artificial categories which objectifying reason tends to apply to matter. Polished marble used as revetments and pavements of Byzantine church interiors, for instance, is part of a long tradition of symbolising water, which its hues and patterns resemble. The play of resemblances and contrasts of the two realities generates a strong metaphoric charge. While this approach may be at odds with the modernist principle of 'truth to materials', it often reveals a deeper, poetic truth.

Parry often describes architectural phenomena through analogy and metaphor, and examples of such a poetic sensibility in the practice's work abound. In the office reception of 7–8 St James's Square,[25] similarly sized panels of rare and precious materials – book-matched American walnut burl veneer and grey-veined Calacatta marble – are juxtaposed as a background to the somewhat theatrical walnut reception desk. An active dialogue is set up between the dense figuration and intense warmth of the dark, curly-patterned wood, and the looser, pale veining and cool reflectivity of the stone. Despite their palpable contrasts, through juxtaposition the substances are revealed as sharing a common origin in the primordial creativity of nature. The architecture thus alludes to the microcosmic tradition expressed, for example, in Baroque cabinets of curiosities. Such a delight in the physicality and thematic content of materials is evident in many of the buildings presented here.[26]

The rich and varied architecture in this volume illustrates how certain philosophical and poetic ideas may be given tangible expression amid the many constraints and pressures of the real world, and even to gain inspiration from them. It is unified in particular by the prioritisation of a coherent urban order over individual predominance and by a focus on the world of concrete experience. Creating buildings belonging to and enhancing a particular place is particularly crucial to counteract the homogenisation and arbitrariness of some branches of contemporary architectural production. An emphasis on high tectonic quality and a kind of making which may be called poetic contributes to an architecture which is useful, durable, and engaging to the senses and the imagination. Building works to last may also be one of the best ways towards the urgent goal of architectural sustainability in these ecologically troubled times. A continuity of these traditions is a means toward authentic renewal. The chapters which follow seek to elucidate some of the practice's recent buildings and projects with reference to these themes.

22   See chapter on Carlton House Terrace in the present volume, pp. 54–65.
23   See André Breton, "Manifesto of Surrealism" (1924) in André Breton, *Manifestoes of Surrealism*, Ann Arbour: University of Michigan Press, 1972.
24   See for example Max Ernst, *The Habit of Leaves*, from *Natural History*, c. 1925, https://www.moma.org/collection/works/94242

25   See Jay Merrick, *Eric Parry Architects Vol 4*, pp. 56–69.
26   See chapters on Carlton House Terrace, pp. 54–65, London Residence, pp. 66–79, and One Chamberlain Square, pp. 80–95 in the present volume.

In Eric Parry Architects' project for Cambridge University Press & Assessment, the west facing side of the reception on the ground floor is greeted by a double-height atrium while the mezzanine space of the first floor holds a collaboration area and café.

e
pa

volume 5

Contents

Fen Court, London

An urbane and very distinctive medium-rise mixed-use building, it combines high-quality office space with exceptionally generous public realm amenities. It is situated at 120 Fenchurch Street, amid the historical fabric of the City of London's financial district, on the south-east edge of the high-rise Eastern Cluster and within sight of the Tower of London. Its unique form was informed by such contextual conditions as the texture of the urban grain and the prevailing building heights in the area, but also by a desire for a certain *joie de vivre*.

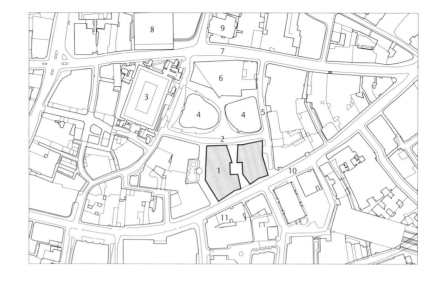

1   Fen Court by Eric Parry Architects
2   Fenchurch Avenue
3   Lloyd's of London by Rogers Strik Harbour + Partners
4   Willis Building by Foster + Partners
5   Billiter Street
6   Diamond Tower by Skidmore, Owings & Merrill
7   Leadenhall Street
8   The Leadenhall Building by Rogers Stirk Harbour + Partners
9   St Andrew Undershaft
10 Fenchurch Street
11 50 Fenchurch Street

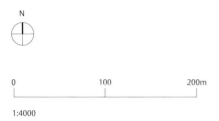

N

0   100   200m

1:4000

Fen Court is a highly inventive addition to the series of Eric Parry Architects' investigations into the architectural potential of the contemporary workplace. Since its opening, it has been enriching many of the daily lives of office workers and local residents, and setting a tone for future developments. An urbane and very distinctive medium-rise mixed-use building, it combines high-quality office space with exceptionally generous public realm amenities. It is situated at 120 Fenchurch Street, amid the historical fabric of the City of London's financial district, on the south-east edge of the high-rise Eastern Cluster and within sight of the Tower of London. Its unique form was informed by such contextual conditions as the texture of the urban grain and the prevailing building heights in the area, but also by a desire for a certain *joie de vivre*. The tripartite structure of the building consists of a double-height base oriented toward the street, a subtly articulated 10-storey body, and a facetted, iridescent glass crown. The base is bisected by a major new walkway with a beguiling art installation, encouraging pedestrian flow across the site. The roof is the site of a spectacular, publicly accessible garden which – together with the new passageway – offers substantial 'planning gains' to the city. Reinterpreting a number of urban traditions, Fen Court presents a vision of the connective and civic role that a contemporary office block can play in the urban public realm.

The site extends between Fenchurch Street to the south and Fenchurch Avenue to the north. The pedestrian lane of Fen Court, with its small public memorial garden, and Billiter Street form its west and east boundaries respectively. The area to the northwest of Fenchurch Avenue is a pedestrian-friendly environment which surrounds the Lloyd's and Willis buildings and leads toward Leadenhall Market. The area's fabric, rooted in the medieval street pattern, is fine grained and pierced by numerous narrow, mostly pedestrian lanes and passageways. One such ancient right of way was Hogarth Court, a dingy alley which – together with Billiter Square – bisected the site. Fenchurch Street Railway Station disgorges into the city a daily stream of commuters, who then make their way on foot through the numerous alleyways to their offices to the north and west of the site area. The preservation of north-south connectivity was therefore an important consideration in the design. Fenchurch Street itself is formed of predominantly medium-height perimeter blocks, to which 20 Fenchurch Street ('the Walkie-Talkie') to the west is a conspicuous exception. The dominant materiality of buildings in the area ranges from traditional Portland stone ashlar and brickwork to various generations of cladding, ranging in colour from blue and green to brown and grey. At the time of the early discussions between the architects and planners, it was felt strongly that the new building should respect the height of the surrounding street, forming

left: Location plan of Eric Parry Architects' Fen Court, between Fenchurch Avenue to the north and Fenchurch Street to the south.

right: South elevation of Fen Court against the City of London skyline in the background.

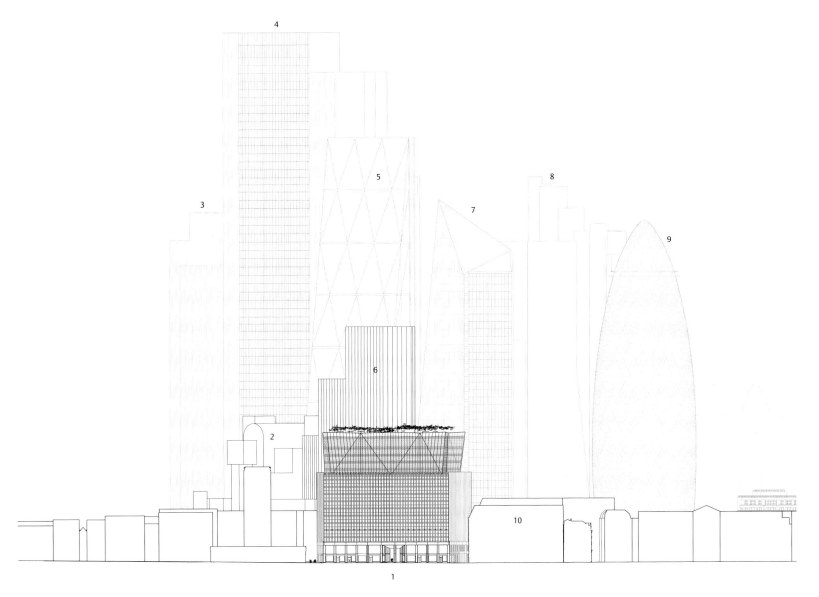

south elevation

1   Eric Parry Architects, Fen Court
2   Lloyd's Building
3   22 Bishopsgate
4   100 Bishopsgate
5   122 Leadenhall Street
6   The Willis Building
7   52–54 Line Street
8   110 Bishopsgate
9   30 St Mary Axe
10 40 Leadenhall Street

0   50m

1:2000

right: View of Fenchurch Street, looking westward towards Fen Court, with 20 Fenchurch Street in the background.

opposite: Eastward view of Fenchurch Avenue towards Fen Court.

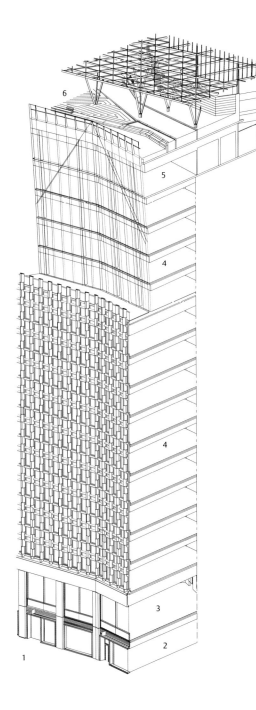

1   Fenchurch Street
2   ground-floor retail
3   ground-floor mezzanine
4   office floors
5   restaurant
6   roof garden

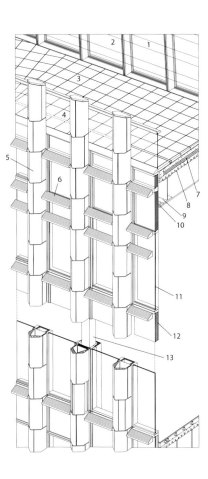

axonometric section

1   275mm interlaminate dichroic band
2   closed cavity façade with external laminated
    single glazing and internal double glazed unit
    (1500mm wide panels)
3   roof terrace
4   glass balustrade
5   ceramic cladding module with joints offseted
    from corners and vertically staggered / mirrored
6   brise-soleil
7   rock wool insulation
8   composite concrete slab
9   primary structural beam
10   recess for roller blind
11   insulated shadow box cladding panel
12   200mm curtain wall unit
13   drylining encasement to structural column

a transition zone – a kind of foothills – to the peak of nearby towers. After a number of iterations, it was decided to work with a mid-rise perimeter block, crowned by another, taller element, set back and forming a distinctive top.

The final scheme is a highly imaginative hybrid. Parry cites such urban precedents as Fritz Höger's Expressionist Chilehaus in Hamburg – a ship-shaped 10-storey office complex, with a public way through, deep interrelated courtyards, and a sculptural parapet oriented toward the sky – to illustrate how architectural variety can be created within a coherent massing and constant height. The highly crafted brick façades of the Chilehaus follow the street with indentations and subtle curves, which create visual interest. The external form of Parry's building likewise follows the geometry of the site. To add dynamism to what would otherwise have been very long, flat elevations, the outer planes of the base and body have been slightly inflected on the north, south and east sides into shallow v-shapes in plan. The west side, similarly angled, follows the boundary of the site. The resulting subtly facetted massing helps visually to break up the large volume of the block and gives the surrounding pavements more generous dimensions. It also modulates the façades and accentuates their corners. The extensive body of the building is thus reduced in bulk and animated. The double-height base is expressed externally by piers and continuous lintels, clad

in polished precast concrete, and framing large-scale vitrines. The old alley of Hogarth Court has been replaced by a newly formed, generous public passageway, bisecting the base of the building and providing an exciting new pedestrian connection. A double-height office reception lobby occupies the north-west corner of the plan, having a suitable relationship with the public realm on Fenchurch Avenue and Fen Court Garden. Major and minor service cores flank the central passageway. The primary, Fenchurch Street frontage is home to four retail units, while the north side contains another two. Loading bays and plant rooms are located in the northeast corner facing Billiter Street, close to the services of the neighbouring buildings. The west side of the building faces onto Fen Court Garden. This tranquil space occupies part of what was once the churchyard of St Gabriel's Fenchurch, a medieval parish church destroyed in the Fire of London. It contains a contemporary granite artwork, the *Gilt of Cain*, which commemorates the activities in this area of the anti-slavery movement. In recognition of the spiritual and contemplative character of this place, the west elevation has no commercial activity and maximises the views of the garden from within.

The most conspicuous feature of the base level is the north-south passageway, which takes the name of the earlier Hogarth Court and accommodates the site's dominant flow. It is focussed on a generously scaled internal space of cubic proportions, which the architects liken

1 restaurant
2 roof garden
3 open air lobby
4 pond
5 skylight

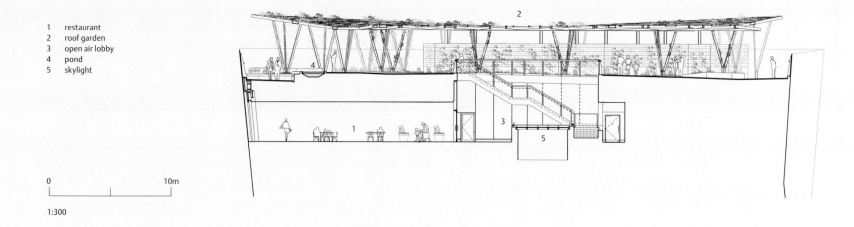

0   10m

1:300

right: Northeastward view of the public garden on the Fen Court roof top, here seen in 2019 soon after the wisteria that was to cover the pergola had been planted.

opposite, above: Section through the restaurant and roof garden including the water feature.

opposite, below: Installation of the pergola with a view of the water feature during construction in February 2018.

to a banking hall. The north and south walkways, which connect this volume with the streets, are splayed out from it in plan. The resulting façade openings afford views through to the street opposite and draw visitors inside. In section, the sloped soffits of the walkways also create a funnel effect, which is accentuated in the southern part by the natural rise of the ground plane. This narrowing toward the central volume creates an exaggerated perspective, a highly theatrical effect reminiscent of some Renaissance and Baroque architecture. The slightly disorienting ambiguity of depth which one experiences on entering accentuates the drama of the passageway and of the mysterious central hall. Fen Court's passageway is a descendant of the nineteenth-century arcades, which developed in order to exploit the commercial potential of inner blocks, transforming them in the process into dream-like worlds of urban *flânerie*.

The term 'banking hall' alludes to the tradition – notable especially in this part of the city – of grand representational rooms, offered by many of the older buildings as part of the civic realm. The size and proportions of the space here are comparable, for example, to those of the great luminous halls of Sir John Soane's Bank of England. In addition to being an urban room, the hall also provides access via dedicated lifts to the 14th-storey restaurant and – importantly – to the roof garden. This central volume replaces a deep atrium of an earlier scheme, which would have been

open to the sky. The flat soffit of the banking hall is covered by a 180m² LED screen, which displays a video art installation that lends the space its drama. Created by artists Vong Phaophanit and Claire Oboussier, this uses lyrical imagery of the surrounding city and sky, accompanied by an eerie and evocative soundtrack. Natural motifs – often drawn from London's parks and waterways – dominate, with an emphasis on the transformations wrought by the changing seasons. There are two cameras located at the roof garden which can be live-streamed to the screen below, creating a a digital-age version of a *camera obscura*. Such devices were sometimes deployed by city spectators as part of the late nineteenth- and early twentieth-century fascination with novel optical technologies. The trend is exemplified by Patrick Geddes' Outlook Tower in Edinburgh. Parry shares this interest in optical phenomena linked to architectural views and sometimes uses them to animate his architecture. The garden's presence is thus vividly announced at street level.

The whole of the passageway is lined with reflective or transparent materials – dark metal panelling, large vitrines and polished black plaster soffits – which bring fragmentary images of the city outside to the mysteriously inflected planes of the interior. The images displayed on the soffit screen bathe the whole passageway in their distorted reflections, and these mingle with fragmentary glimpses of the outer world. The overall effect is enticing and mysterious. It brings to mind the

mid-twentieth-century experimental theatre of the *laterna magica* in which still and moving images projected on stage sets or smoke were combined with live action in an ambiguous and richly textured collagist whole. The ceiling imagery of the banking hall, generally shot in the vertical direction, also creates a compelling sense of an open sky above. The changing scenery on the soffit screen is reflected by the adjacent vertical glazing in a way which gives the illusion of the 'sky' spreading out beyond the hall's enclosure, melting it, and setting off a cubistic play of flatness and depth. Some of the most effective video scenes are those of looking up into tree crowns or down onto gently rippling water surfaces, conjuring up spatial ambiguities and a distant memory of the motif of heavenly grottoes in the bowels of the earth. With all these possible readings, the banking hall can be seen as an allusion to the architectural tradition of the cosmic room. Even on repeat visits, the experience is mesmerising.

Above the base, the main body of the building comprises nine storeys of high-spec office space. The deep atrium which pierced the floor plates of an early proposal has been removed, and most of the structure is contained in the envelope. This allows for a highly efficient and flexible floor plate. This portion of the building, a kind of plinth, is likened by the architects to its shouldered body. It is externally expressed by a façade of fine ribs of engaged piers at 3-metre centres, projecting slightly beyond the surface of the glazing, and clad in luminous off-white

glazed ceramic, fabricated by Darwen. Most of the ceramic components used here are extruded in 1-metre lengths. These are combined with scalloped accent pieces, which were cast. The spaces between the ribs are spanned by polychromatic aluminium *brise-soleil*, giving a horizontal rhythm. The subtle inflections of the façades' planes gave rise to many varying joint conditions, so the cladding at each junction has a slightly different detail. Combined with the depth of the projecting elements, the facets seem to vary in colour and mass, yet form part of a consistent whole. Viewed obliquely, they can appear almost solid, but seem to open up when seen more head on. This lends visual subtlety and allows more daylight to reach the lower levels. The ceramic ribs terminate in a spiky parapet at the level of the 11th-floor terrace.

Parry's work with glazed ceramic blocks is in part informed by the context; interesting examples of ceramic façades in the area include H. P. Berlage's Holland House and the Art Nouveau Bolton House. The main reason for his frequent choice of this durable material, however, are the subtleties of colour, texture and light modulation it affords. At the Holburne Museum, for example, the extension's dappled, shimmering finish was painstakingly selected to reflect and resonate with the foliage of the landscape garden in which it is sited. At Fen Court, the neutral colour of the ceramic ranges between white and grey, the pale hue helping to reflect light down into the surrounding streets.

above: Recent views of the garden with the growing wisteria and detail of the seating.

right: Axonometric of the cityscape to the north of Fenchurch Street, showing a sequence of building heights and roof tops descending to the height of the Fen Court roof garden. To the south of Fen Court and west of Fenchurch Street train station is the anticipated public realm of Eric Parry Architects' 50 Fenchurch Street.

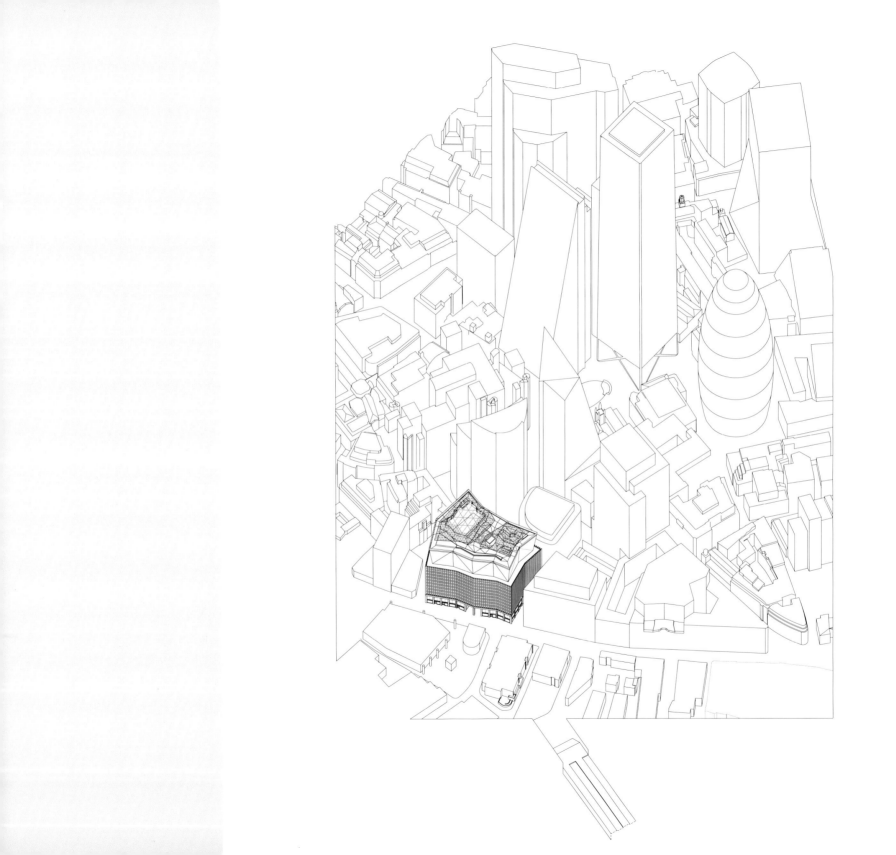

Above the shoulder horizon of the tenth floor, the building is dramatically transformed from a restrained urban block to an exuberantly sculptural form, a kind of crystalline crown. This iridescent 5-storey section, which contains further offices and a restaurant, is widely visible from different points in the city and joyfully acknowledges its connection with the sky. It is set back slightly, creating a terrace, and splayed out towards the top. The outer surfaces here are made from a highly transparent and energy-efficient glass, closed-cavity façade. The complex geometries which resulted from its being inclined and folded in triangular facets required a high level of expertise and precision on the part of the façade contractor. The glazing here is made with an interlayer of dichroic foils. These accentuate reflections of the sky and surrounding buildings. The resulting rich iridescence is due to a striking optical effect, where white light is split into beams of differing wavelengths, making objects appear to fluctuate between two colours. The same phenomenon is observable in nature, as in the changeable metallic gleam of beetles or hummingbirds. Here it has the startling consequence of making the vitreous planes shimmer in a dramatic range of colours, from blue-green to violet-pink. Parry sees this playful polychromy as an antidote to the "cadaverous green of glass" which dominates much of the city. It gives the building a distinctive presence on the skyline.

The publicly accessible roof garden – the most fortuitous product of negotiations with the City of London planners – is an important component of the building's contribution to the life of the city. The result of a 2008 competition, the garden was designed by the German landscape firm Latz + Partner in collaboration with Eric Parry Architects. The chief aim was to develop the roof as an amenity which would provide a restorative natural retreat in the middle of the City's office landscape through a stimulation of the senses. Enclosed by a balustrade of clear glass, the garden is encircled by a perimeter walk, offering exciting panoramic views of the surrounding city. Its vast lattice canopies are laden with the boughs and the scented pinkish-blue flower clusters of 80 wisteria trees – several species were used to maximise the blooming period – resembling clouds and providing shelter from sun and rain. The soft planting creates dramatic contrasts with the hard materials and angular forms of the landscaping and plant rooms. This very civic space makes a significant addition to the recreational facilities of this part of the city, and has become a much loved destination for office workers, visitors and local residents. Roof gardens and viewing platforms of various kinds have since been written into planning policy for all future tall buildings in the City of London, as part of the Corporation's goal of 'urban greening'.

left: Sequence of concatenated surfaces along the Fenchurch Street façade reflecting the variety of colours that result from the midday light.

right: Northward view of Fen Court Garden with Fen Court on the right.

30 St James's Square

In recent years, the area to the north of St James's Square has been the site of two other major projects by Eric Parry Architects. One Eagle Place and 7–8 St James's Square each reconstituted the urban fabric with high-quality contemporary architecture. Both of these were carefully crafted ensembles which – in their functions, massing and public faces – responded to aspects of their historic urban context and set an example for sensitive future development. These principles also apply to 30 St James's Square, which forms the east end of a terrace, addressing both the elegant square to the north and the broad avenue of Pall Mall to the south.

1 Eric Parry Architects' 30 St James's Square
2 Eric Parry Architects' 7–8 St James's Square
3 Eric Parry Architects' One Eagle Place, Piccadilly
4 Eric Parry Architects' 15 and 20 Jermyn Street and 27 Regent Street
5 St James's Square
6 Pall Mall
7 Charles II Street
8 Duke of York Street
9 Jermym Street
10 Piccadilly
11 Waterloo Place
12 Regent Street

N

0 10 25   50   100m

1:4000

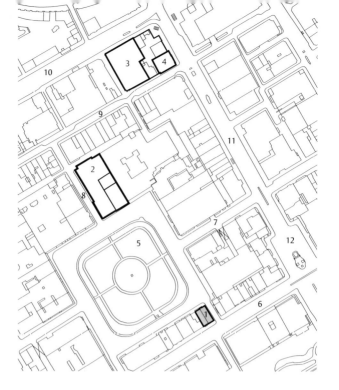

30 St James's Square is a very different kind of office building from Fen Court. Due to its exceptionally sensitive location, the focus of the design here was on the exterior, an exploration of the role that façades play in the legibility and continuity of urban fabric. It is situated at the heart of the St James's Conservation Area in Westminster. The area has a very rich history, traditional links with the British establishment, and a character of refined exclusivity. Eric Parry Architects was brought in to upgrade the property, which consisted of two interconnected office blocks, 21 and 22 Pall Mall. Built around the turn of the twentieth century, these had been joined in an unsatisfactory 1980s remodelling. After an initial assessment, the practice decided to erect a unified new structure across the two plots within the retained and remodelled historical façades. The building was extended with the addition of a new floor of office space, lifting the cornice line to align with that of nearby buildings and providing the terrace with a fitting terminal. The small size of the floor plates necessitated astute internal organisation to create highly desirable, contemporary office space. The deep sensitivities of the site area required a careful consideration of the local character and precedents, and a superior quality of execution.

In recent years, the area to the north of St James's Square has been the site of two other major projects by Eric Parry Architects. One Eagle Place and 7–8 St James's Square each reconstituted the urban fabric with high-quality contemporary architecture [See Volume 4]. Both of these were carefully crafted ensembles which – in their functions, massing and public faces – responded to aspects of their historic urban context and set an example for sensitive future development. These principles also apply to 30 St James's Square, which forms the east end of a terrace, addressing both the elegant square to the north and the broad avenue of Pall Mall to the south. The project is also an exemplary study in how sympathetically to upgrade and modify an existing façade.

The historic district of St James's remains one of the most prestigious areas of London. Due to its proximity to the palaces of Whitehall and St James's, and to the seat of government at Westminster, it had historically been associated with the royal court and the upper echelons of society. St James's Square was at the heart of an exclusive residential development, laid out in the last decades of the seventeenth century by Henry Jermyn, 1st Earl of St Albans, after he had been granted the land by Charles II. The spire of Christopher Wren's St James's church overlooked the scheme from the north and was for a long time the most prominent feature in the area. One of the oldest residential squares in London, St James's Square was (with Inigo Jones' Covent Garden Piazza) a model for countless subsequent Georgian developments. Its east, north and west sides were built up first, with exceptionally grand townhouses on deep plots. Its south side, forming the boundary between the square and Pall Mall (so named after a royal ball game which had been played there), comprised smaller, more modest plots with two aspects. These would be the first in the square to be turned to commercial uses. During

opposite, left: Location plan of 30 St James's Square by the southeast of the square, including to the north also designed by Eric Parry Architects, 7–8 St James's Square as well as One Eagle Place, Piccadilly, 15 and 20 Jermyn Street, and 27 Regent Street.

opposite, right: Southeastern view of the pre-existing buildings from St James's Square towards Pall Mall.

above: View of the pre-existing buildings as seen from Pall Mall. The façades were considerably shorter and at variance with the height of the neighbouring buildings and the remaining urban fabric.

right: Northwestward view of 30 St James's Square from Pall Mall, showing the entirely renovated brick and stone façades, which were extended upwards to meet the cornice lines of the neighbouring buildings, and topped by the dormers of an also newly completed roof.

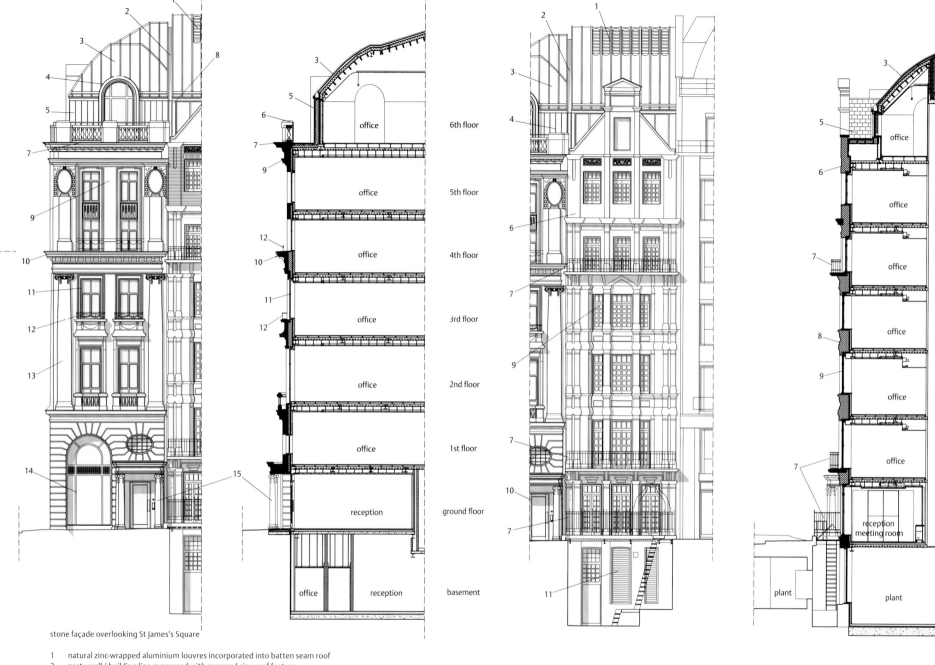

stone façade overlooking St James's Square

1 natural zinc-wrapped aluminium louvres incorporated into batten seam roof
2 party wall / building line expressed with recessed zinc roof feature
3 batten seam natural zinc roof with zinc fascia, soffit and concealed gutter
4 prefabricated internally soldered zinc arched dormers
5 natural zinc double lock standing seam wall
6 new galvanised and painted metal balustrade with patinated bronze handrail
7 pre-existing cornice and balustrade reconstructed as part of the additional storey
8 removable natural zinc wall panels
9 additional storey in solid Portland stone with reused elements from pre-existing façade
10 new Portland stone cornice
11 new metal casement windows
12 all metalwork including railings and balustrades removed, repaired and painted
13 pre-existing stone and brick façade retained, repaired and cleaned
14 patinated bronze shopfront windows using newly milled and integrated profiles
15 relocated entrance portico with reused columns

brick façade overlooking St James's Square

1 natural zinc-wrapped aluminium louvres incorporated into batten seam roof
2 party wall / building line expressed with recessed zinc roof feature
3 batten seam natural zinc roof with zinc fascia, soffit and concealed gutter
4 natural zinc double lock standing seam wall
5 new Welsh slate roof as H62/150 to retained gable
6 additional storey in solid handmade brickwork and new or reused red sandstone
7 all metalwork including railings and balustrades removed, repaired and painted
8 pre-existing stone and brick façade retained, repaired and cleaned
9 new timber casement windows with low iron double glazing
10 relocated entrance portico with reused columns
11 new metal louvred openings to plant rooms

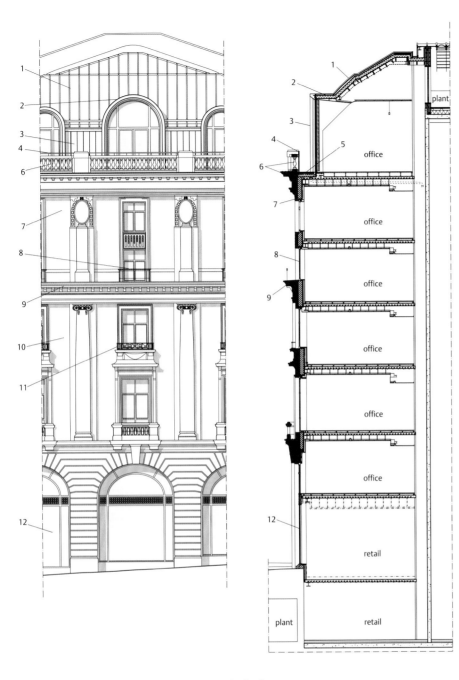

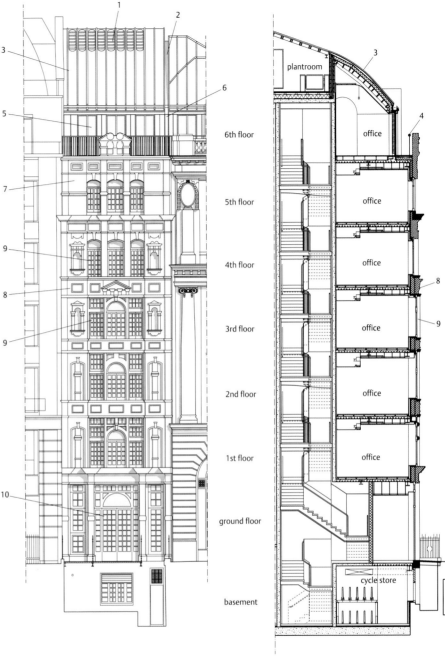

stone façade to the east between St James's Square and Pall Mall

1   batten seam natural zinc roof with zinc fascia
2   prefabricated internally soldered zinc arched dormers
3   natural zinc double lock standing seam wall
4   new galvanised and painted metal balustrade with patinated bronze handrail
5   inverted roof terrace
6   pre-existing cornice and balustrade reconstructed as part of the additional storey
7   additional storey in solid Portland stone with reused elements from pre-existing façade
8   new metal casement windows
9   new Portland stone cornice
10 pre-existing stone and brick façade retained, repaired and cleaned
11 all metalwork including railings and balustrades removed, repaired and painted
12 patinated bronze shopfront windows using newly milled and integrated profiles

brick façade overlooking Pall Mall

1   natural zinc-wrapped aluminium louvres incorporated into batten seam roof
2   party wall / building line expressed with recessed zinc roof feature
3   batten seam natural zinc roof with zinc fascia, soffit and concealed gutter
4   new galvanised and painted metal balustrade with patinated bronze handrail
5   natural zinc double lock standing seam wall
6   removable natural zinc wall panels
7   additional storey in solid handmade brickwork with new and reused red sandstone
8   pre-existing stone and brick façade retained, repaired and cleaned
9   new timber casement windows with low ion double glazing
10   new rear entrance and fire exit doors

1:200

the eighteenth century, St James's Square, with its lamp-lit polygonal enclosure around a large basin, served as an outdoor recreation and display room for the nobility and gentry, and contained many aristocratic residences. The later eighteenth century saw some of these townhouses being modified and converted to other uses. By the mid-nineteenth century, the elite occupiers included a number of private members' clubs, embassies, financial and diplomatic institutions, and the London Library. Pall Mall had become an exclusive, fashionable shopping street.

The grid of streets around St James's Square has remained essentially unchanged since the seventeenth century. It is characterised by a clear hierarchy, ranging from the honorific square itself and the spacious thoroughfare of Pall Mall to dignified, residentially scaled streets and the more modest grain of mews and yards. The area contains a large number of notable and listed buildings, many by Britain's leading architects. These include 20 St James's Square by Robert Adam, Royal Opera Arcade and Carlton House Terrace by John Nash, the Travellers and Reform clubs by Charles Barry, and the Economist Plaza by Alison and Peter Smithson. During the Blitz the area suffered bomb damage, which gave rise to a few over-scaled modern buildings. It remains today the home of many of the institutions of the establishment, interspersed with financial corporations and art galleries. The requisite character for new buildings in this sensitive area is one of restrained

elegance, respect for architectural traditions, and a high quality of materials and craftsmanship.

30 St James's Square consists of two historical plots – 21 and 22 Pall Mall – at the east end of the terrace forming the southern boundary of the square. The two buildings, built about 30 years apart, were combined into one in the 1980s, when the interior was demolished behind the retained façades. The subsequent reconstruction fell short in a number of areas, leading to a building which was inefficient, poorly accessible and marred by awkward relationships between the serviced floor slabs and fenestration. Upgrading it to modern standards was badly needed. An investigation by Eric Parry Architects determined that the best solution was again completely to reconstruct the interior, conserving and modifying the envelopes. As these were lower than adjacent properties, a permission was obtained to add a level to the new building, extending the façades, lifting the cornice and tidying up the roofscape. A new core was built in the centre of the plan near the western party wall and a hybrid steel frame and in-situ reinforced concrete structure was inserted. As the floor plates of the original buildings had been at slightly different levels from each other, careful calibration was required to optimise the relationships between the thinner new floor slabs and the exterior openings, so that a level entry could be provided to all office floors and more generous floor-to-ceiling heights created. An additional office floor was added and both

left: Hand drawing by Eric Parry for 30 St James's Square, dating from 2015, which suggests a significant rise in the height of the stone façade, crowned by the continuous undulating surface of a new roof top.

above: Initial wooden model for 30 St James's Square, displaying the early proposal for the roof covering the new top floors. The stone façade was here increased by one floor, matching the height of the brick façade, which still retained its height and gabled shape.

opposite: Completed office reception, featuring Eric Parry Architects' design for the reception desk.

façades extended. New zinc-clad mansard roofs unify the two retained envelopes, while also hinting at their historic independence.

Number 21, the east end of the terrace, was built for automobile maker Renault by Edward Boehmer in 1911. Its three Portland stone façades are in the Beaux-Arts style, which has numerous precedents in the area, most notably in the contemporaneous Royal Automobile Club on the opposite side of Pall Mall. The large, double-height arched openings at ground level recall the building's original use as an automobile showroom. By contrast, Number 22 was built in the prevailing Victorian style for the Imperial Insurance Company by Osborn and Russell in 1880. The whole building has been reglazed in low-iron glazing in frames of steel, patinated bronze or timber, as appropriate to each façade.

The office reception area, with a new glazed entrance screen, is located on the principal elevation, facing St James's Square. A stone Ionic porch, which had been widened and moved to the corner of the building in the 1980s, has been re-established in its original location, marking the office entry and allowing for a better plan resolution. The coarse recent stone ornamentation has been removed and the porch restored, using most of the original stonework. Behind the square frontage, the well-proportioned office reception has an adjoining meeting room. They are connected by a large opening with sliding full-height panels, which make it possible for the meeting room to be closed off and used for separate functions. Both deploy fine and highly crafted natural materials and refined detailing to achieve an atmosphere of elegance and exclusivity. Their interior design takes its cues from the different fenestration of the two conserved façades. The reception is a larger, nearly square space, with full-height, bronze-framed windows. The main feature here is the highly sculptural, patinated bronze reception desk, with its wide fluting and undulating curved top. The full-height banquette and the sliding door panels are covered in grey horse-hair fabric. A highly crafted, glossy, French-grey lacquer is used here on the fluted and reveal wall panels. Providing continuity throughout the public areas of the building (including in the lift lobbies, toilets, and on door architraves) the lacquer panels are immaculately detailed and provide a durable finish of great refinement.

The meeting room has a more enclosed, private feeling. Here the windows echo the forms of the original casements, with small panes in white-painted timber frames. The higher cill-to-floor dimension of the windows enables their recesses to be used as leather-upholstered, patinated bronze seats. The two rooms subtly suggest their different origins, yet are connected through a coherent language of materials and detailing. The recurring use of the fluting motif unifies all the public areas of the building, while also making a stylised refence to the classical tradition. As with the external treatment of the conserved façades, there is a feeling here both of distinct places and of a unified whole.

The numerous elements of the interior are brought together in a skilful and efficient way. The main stair is made of welded steel plate, with stone-clad steps and highly crafted wooden handrails. The lift lobbies receive daylight from the east and are entirely lined with grey lacquer panels, with patinated-bronze lift doors and bronze door handles. The new layout has optimised the arrangement of the office floor plates, which are now U-shaped and flexible, with clear spans and views in three directions. The typical distance of six metres between the operable windows and the core ensures the high levels of daylight and natural ventilation required for boutique offices. Perhaps the most dramatic of these is at the top level, where the tall mansard roof, set back from the line of remodelled façades and concealing the plant room at the top, creates an interesting section with extra ceiling height and a play of light on sloping wall surfaces. The tall openings look over the perimeter roof terrace and offer spectacular views across the rooftops.

The remodelling of the retained façades is perhaps the most noteworthy part of the project. The Victorian Number 22 has elevations of red brick, accented with yellow and red sandstone cornices, and inset sandstone and carved brick ornamentation. The principal front facing the square has full-width balconies with metal railings at *piano nobile* and mid-rise cornice levels. There are lightwells with railings at ground level of both fronts, with an access bridge on Pall Mall. Brick piers and string courses frame the fenestration in a tripartite order. The elevations had been

extended in the 1980s reconstruction, when the gables were added. This extension was, however, poorly matched to the tone and texture of the original brick. In the new building this has been corrected with the use of carefully coordinated handmade brick. The original sandstone features were cleaned and reused. In raising the Pall Mall façade, a simple facsimile storey was constructed in place of the 1980s gable, with the original flat parapet crowned by its pediment. On the St James's Square side, the gable was retained and reconstructed a storey higher. Roofed in Welsh slate, it incorporates some of the salvaged elements and is again capped with the original pediment.

At Number 21, the end of the terrace, the three highly ornate Portland stone façades in the Beaux-Arts style comprise the typical three levels of the base, *piano nobile* and attic. The rusticated ground base contains double-height arched openings, modified by the insertion of a mezzanine just below the arch. The four arches on the south and east elevations have sculpted keystones depicting mythical figures. These include Hermes, the herald of the gods associated with travel, and the blacksmith god Hephaestus, the patron of manufacture. They thus relate thematically to the iconography of the original owner, Renault. The first and second storeys are articulated as a *piano nobile*, connected by giant-order Ionic pilasters below a mid-rise cornice. The windows have Juliet balconies with stone balustrades or metal railings. Above this the attic was originally single storey, its windows framed by pilasters. These were capped with plain oval roundels, hung with

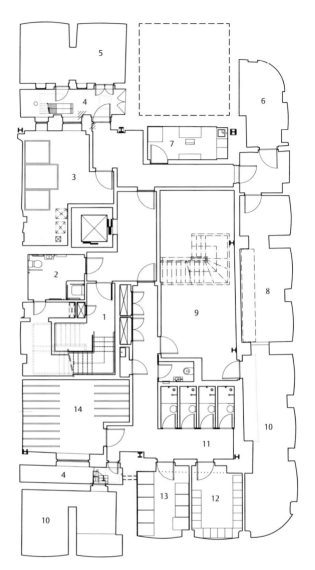

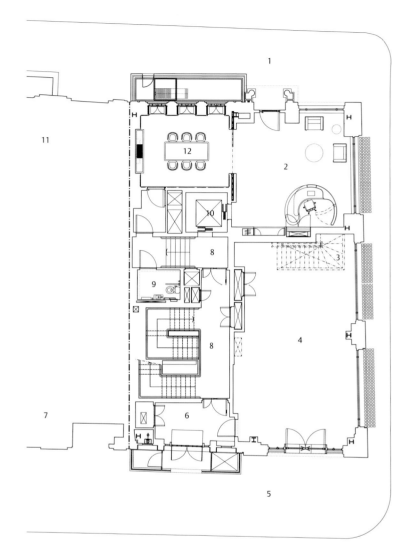

basement

1 stair
2 accessible wc
3 vent plant room
4 lightwell
5 life safety generator
6 switch room
7 office
8 pumps and water tank room
9 retail office
10 retail store
11 showers and wc
12 lockers
13 bin store
14 bicycle store (28 spaces)

ground-floor plan

1 St James's Square
2 office reception
3 future retail stair
4 retail
5 Pall Mall
6 entrance
7 23–24 Pall Mall
8 stairs
9 disabled wc
10 lift
11 28–29 St James's Square
12 meeting room

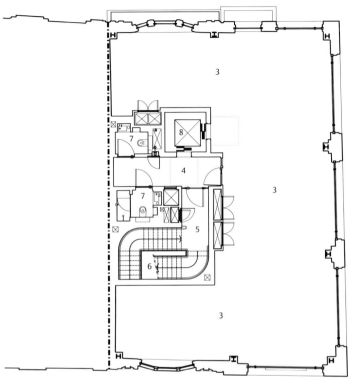

first floor plan

1   St James's Square
2   Pall Mall
3   office
4   lift lobby
5   stair lobby
6   stairs
7   wc
8   lift

sixth floor plan

1   St James's Square
2   Pall Mall
3   office
4   lift lobby
5   stair lobby
6   plant access
7   stair
8   wc
9   lift

0   5m

1:200

N

garlands, below a cornice and a bottle balustrade. The previous roof was a setback mansard with arched dormers.

In adding the new office floor to Number 21, the upper section above the mid-rise cornice was extended using carefully matched Portland stone ashlar. To find the closest match, the design team visited Albion Stone's mine in Dorset, which had been its original source. The medium-grained Jordans Whitbread limestone was selected. The new windows of the new storey are framed within vertical panels with the ones immediately below, from which they are separated by new stone spandrels. These large new ashlar blocks are carved with floral ornament, complementing the original garlands above and Ionic capitals below. The framing of this upper section by the extended pilasters, which have now also become a giant order, has a major precedent in John Nash's nearby Waterloo Place. It integrates the taller new attic level seamlessly into the façade composition. It is now closer in height to the base and *piano nobile* sections below, giving the façade better proportions. Office levels 2 to 5 are thus discreetly integrated into a satisfying hierarchical external order. The raised cornice is continuous with Number 22 and is again surmounted by the adapted bottle balustrade. The new mansard roof contains five prefabricated round-arched, barrel-vaulted zinc dormers, which echo the form of the base level arches.

The practice's original scheme for the building had been capped by a luminous lantern roof, with large areas of clerestory glazing below a curvilinear ceramic parasol, floating high above and uniting the two halves. In discussions with planners, however, it was deemed to be too bright and contemporary for the area. A solution was adopted of more traditional zinc standing-seam mansard roofs, unpatinated for gradual weathering. Each half of the roof takes its forms from the retained façades below: Beaux-Arts arched dormers for Number 21 and a simple double-pitched mansard over clerestory fenestration for Number 22. The dormers were prefabricated by VMZINK, whose zinc roofs and dormers give the roofscapes of Baron Haussmann's Parisian boulevards their characteristic bluish tinge. The original building line between the two halves is expressed as a recessed zinc feature, marking where the party wall once stood and preserving a spectral memory of the original grain of townhouse plots. Despite being less playful than the original proposal, the present roof solution is simple and refined, concealing the western party wall and bringing an intelligible order to the roofscape.

The meticulous, sensitive remodelling of the retained façades at 30 St James's Square indicates an understanding of the importance of the communicative face of a building as part of an intelligible urban order. The project was again informed by an empathy with the context, but it also sets an example of a nuanced approach to renewal within the situational setting of the London street and square. The design plays with the tension between the parts and whole, the original two buildings coming together into one.

above: Four sculpted keystones. Far left: Hermes or Mercury, god of communication, facing Pall Mall, frequently idolised in corners or junctions of the cities of Antiquity. Three keystones facing the street connecting Pall Mall to St James's Square: first, Daphne or an androgynous figure of Apollo as equally signified by the laurel wreath; second, a clear allusion to industry in the image of Hephaestus or Vulcan, blacksmith of the gods and brother to both Hermes and Apollo, also a possible reference to the three Renault brothers, who founded the Société Renault Frères; and third, Hera or Juno, mother to Hephaestus and goddess of counsel and family.

right: External view of the office reception facing St James's Square.

Carlton House Terrace

Carlton House Terrace is a highly prestigious street in the St James's District of the City of Westminster, and a short distance from St James's Square. The pre-existing structure is part of the two Regency terraces built by John Nash between 1827 and 1832. These replaced Carlton House, the royal palace which had been the terminal of Nash's great Regent Street urban development. The terraces' palatial, neoclassical bulk overlooks St James's Park to the south, and provides an appropriately grand, scenographic background to the ceremonial route of the Mall.

Eric Parry Architects was appointed to carry out the major refurbishment to a Grade 1-listed Regency townhouse at Carlton House Terrace in 2015, after it had been acquired by an international financial institution for its London headquarters. In this type of workplace, the design focus was on the restrained luxury and somewhat oneiric atmosphere of a mostly hidden, interior world. Carlton House Terrace is a highly prestigious street in the St James's District of the City of Westminster, and a short distance from St James's Square. The pre-existing structure is part of the two Regency terraces built by John Nash between 1827 and 1832. These replaced Carlton House, the royal palace which had been the terminal of Nash's great Regent Street urban development. The terraces' palatial, neoclassical bulk overlooks St James's Park to the south, and provides an appropriately grand, scenographic background to the ceremonial route of the Mall. The more formal south façades have giant-order Corinthian columnar screens, central pediments with stucco scrollwork and higher end pavilions. As with Nash's grand terraces around Regent's Park, the buildings are clad and ornamented in consistent cream stucco, and this deliberate uniformity subordinates the individual character of the constituent houses to that of the single palatial edifice. These were originally the townhouses of aristocratic families and numerous statesmen, and contained a variety of splendid interiors, expressive of the residents' status and taste. More recently, many have housed learned societies. This particular house, which had suffered serious bomb damage

in the Blitz, had been the home of the Royal College of Pathologists. The last major refurbishment, which took place in 1967, turned most of its interior to open-plan office space. The challenge for the practice was to modernise and reconfigure the tired interiors around plentiful natural light, so as to provide an appropriately dignified and distinctive London home for a modern financial company and a portion of its extensive art collection. The transformation had to occur without any changes to the iconic façades, with which the new interior had to retain a meaningful relationship. This was achieved by converting an old court into a light-filled atrium and wintergarden with a feature suspended staircase, around which the programme is logically organised, and by reconfiguring the plan to create more interesting spaces relating to those of the original form of the house. The potential of the roofscapes has been fully exploited with a new sun pavilion and terrace, offering spectacular views of the Westminster skyline. Elegant contemporary accommodation has been created within the parameters of a historic fabric.

The entrance of the house is up through a heavy Doric porch across the usual lightwell into a generous reception space. The flooring at ground level is of grey and white stone in an orthogonal pattern, which recalls traditional precedents. The other half of the street frontage contains an elegant meeting room with a coved ceiling, whose dramatic lights recall an astronomical chart. One of the ways

left: Southward view of Waterloo Place, with John Henry Foley's sculpture of Sidney Herbert in the foreground as part of the broader monumental programme of the area, which also includes a number of war monuments; behind it, the famous clubhouse, The Athenæum, designed by Decimus Burton; in the background, Benjamin Dean Wyatt's towering column monumentalising Sir Richard Westmacott's sculpture of Prince Frederick, Duke of York and Albany; next to it, Sir Bertam Mackennal's equestrian sculpture of Edward VII; and also in the background, John Nash's Carlton House Terrace buildings for The Royal Society.

right: Site plan of the Carlton House Terrace area with an indication of the exact sites that were hit during the Blitz and the level of damage to urban fabric and interiors of buildings at the end of WWII.

overleaf: The new interior of Carlton House Terrace, one of John Nash's townhouses, now the London HQ of an international financial institution, designed by Eric Parry Architects.

of providing a consistency and a sophisticated modern aura to the disparate rooms and openings of the house is through the use of exquisite light-grey lacquer detailing. It frames all the openings and covers doors, sliding panels, media cabinetry, skirting boards and the reeded panels which form a dado to many of the rooms. The colour palette resounds with the Regency exterior and provides an understated background to the artworks. The ground level contains four well-appointed meeting and conference rooms of different sizes and represents the most public face of the company.

The reception leads to the stair lobby, which also holds the lift, fire stairs and toilets. The grand staircase and stucco-relief decorations here have been conserved in their post-war restored form, with dramatic new lighting and a dark green carpet, which foreshadows the wintergarden beyond. Traversing the stair hall, one arrives at the base of the new atrium, which acts as a focal point around which the building is organised. An enormously tall space finished in luminous polished plaster, it fills the deep interior with natural light, and provides visual connectivity. It is formed by the curved projecting east wall of the old ante-room and by the flowing curvature of the new stair and gallery above on the west side. The stone floor contains glazed panels which filter daylight into the lower-ground area. The atrium contains a suspended structure reminiscent of a modernist mobile: a hanging garden with abundant vegetation. The

cascading sequence of seven white metal planters is asymmetrical and counterweighted, connected by orthogonal balance-like steel beams, cables and a curvilinear irrigation line. On the lowest level, a sculptural metal basin on a stone base terminates the vertical sequence and receives any overflow, completing the water's journey, as it were, from the sky to the earth. The metal structure of the hanging garden echoes the stair handrail. It recalls the craft of the blacksmith, present in Georgian and Regency architecture in the ubiquitous metal railings. The ground level of the atrium adjoins the two conference rooms and provides something of a public forum.

The first floor, a *piano nobile* which originally held the reception and drawing rooms, contains the company's principal offices. Here a number of walls removed in recent refurbishments have been reinstated, creating a plan of implicit rooms, better attuned to the original character of the house. Three individual executive offices face the leafy street frontage. The two partitions which divide them each consist of a central solid panel flanked by panels of clear glass, containing doors on the south side. The lower half of each partition generally comprises ash veneer cabinetry. The flanking glazing recalls an *enfilade* arrangement and the transparency creates a sense of spatial continuity. The detailing of these rooms – the consistent lacquer framing and continuous strip light recess, for example – gives the impression of the three offices as part of one grand space.

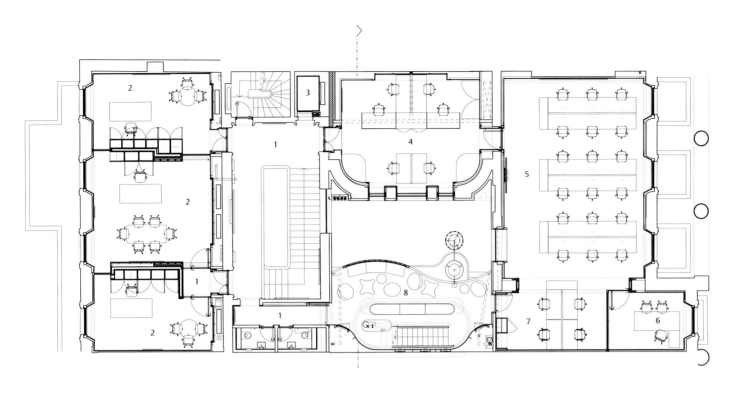

first floor

1 lobby
2 executive office
3 lift
4 European Fund Managers & PAs
5 fund managers
6 office
7 office / breakout
8 tea point

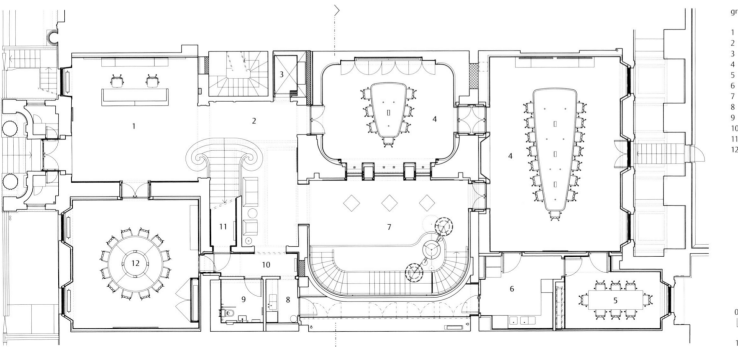

ground floor

1 reception
2 lobby
3 lift
4 conference rooms
5 annex
6 kitchen
7 winter garden
8 tea point
9 accessible wc
10 lobby
11 luggage store
12 meeting room

N

0   5m

1:200

The fund managers' office occupies what would have been the grandest room in the mansion, the former drawing room. The three lofty sash windows here look out across the Mall to the greenery of St James's Park from behind the enormous Corinthian capitals of the façade colonnade, giving access to balconies. As elsewhere, this monumental space is given human scale and consistent detailing with the lacquer reeded dado panels and frames around openings. The west bay, which extends beyond the office wall to the columnar screen, also echoes the original arrangement as a formal *poché* annex. An interesting tension is thus set up in many of the old reception rooms between the containment of a discrete volume and the flowing, modern space of a contemporary office landscape.

On the first level, the atrium contains a curved gallery with pale wood oak parquet flooring, a tea point and built-in leather seating. Bathed in natural light, it provides an informal staff meeting place. A surprisingly transparent floor light accentuates the sense of a high perch and allows light to filter to lower levels. The chief feature here is the suspended steel staircase on the west side. It is fabricated from 20mm steel plate and painted white to suggest lightness, its steps lined with timber. Detached from the wall and suspended on slender steel cables so that it does not touch the floor, it appears to hover weightlessly in the air. The balustrade is made of enormous sheets of clear glass, the end ones curved. This heightens the sense of dematerialisation. The dark metal

handrails seem to dance around the black suspension cables, creating a sense of movement. The subtle S-curve of the gallery edge echoes the movement of the stair, while also responding to the outward curve of the old ante-room opposite. The pots of cascading greenery also appeal to levitate and conjure up a vibrant tropical garden in the middle of London. The wintergarden and stair thus confound expectations. Their surprising, vaguely surreal effect is one of cultivated artificiality.

Ascending the hanging stair and rising above the atrium roof, one reaches the second floor. Here, on what would originally have been the level of family bedrooms, the scale and mood become more domestic. The offices are less grand and the entire south frontage is devoted to the principal's private apartment. Separated from the office world by acoustic isolation lobbies, it is a small, sumptuous world unto itself. Situated above the façade colonnade, it is flooded with sunlight. A heavy metal door with bespoke handles opens into a reception room of contemporary sophistication. A small kitchen is faced with black and white marble, and dominated by a polished stainless steel unit, which can be converted from a pristine cuboid to a kitchen island and bar seating. Lacquer panels here also become shutters. Other colours in the apartment are more saturated, with oak flooring, smoked oak shelving and cabinetry, and burgundy lacquer on the tall interior door which separates the more public realm of the apartment from the most private. Some doors can close in one of two positions, changing the configuration of the space.

above, from left to right (see plans on p. 59): First, view from the ground-floor reception (1) into the lobby (2), looking towards the lift (3) and the conference room on the left (4) and the winter garden on the right (7); second and third, the executive offices on the first floor (2); fourth, the conference room (4) as seen from the ground-floor lobby; fifth, the fund managers room on the first floor (5); sixth, the corner office on the first floor (6).

In addition to further office space and plant rooms, the third floor contains comfortable, south-facing accommodation for visiting staff. This projecting bay, which originally had been a *poché* adjunct to the principal rooms, lost this identity in the previous open-plan office arrangement and is here restored with a partition wall. The salon, located in the old curved ante-room on the east side, is a staff social hub. It contains a spiral staircase which gives access to a new sun pavilion and terrace on the roof. Facing St James's Park, this roof garden provides a congenial place to relax, with privileged panoramic views over London and many of the institutions of its political power.

The restraint and relative anonymity of the exterior of the Regency townhouse, contrasted with its often sumptuous and highly individual interior, can perhaps be compared to another period of history. Many *fin de siècle* European cities, such as Brussels or Vienna, saw the brief flowering of Art Nouveau. This movement was informed by a growing interest in new industrial technologies and exquisitely detailed and crafted materials, yet it also sought a symbolic language of cultural renewal. The bourgeois home sometimes became an evocation of the introverted, private psychic and dream world of the individual. In Symbolist literature, which inspired Art Nouveau, elements of the natural world were deliberately and fantastically transformed – made strange – through artistic artifice. Eric Parry has made a close study

of the architecture of the Belgian Art Nouveau architect Victor Horta, whose beautifully crafted, sensual and very artificial interior worlds are of enduring interest. He mentions the architect's atmospheric Hôtel Tassel as having been at the back of his mind during this project. Horta's townhouse had used a wintergarden linked with a staircase and filled with exuberant metal, fresco and mosaic ornamentation to bring light and exoticism to the interior. The abundance of fantastic whiplash curves of the wrought-iron capitals, balustrades, floor mosaics and wall paintings, drawn from vegetal forms, was meant to suggest the fusion of crafts and nature. The knowing artificiality at Carlton House Terrace of the wintergarden, the dematerialised staircase and the cocooned, sumptuous intimacy of the principal's apartment arguably recall some of Horta's architectural sensibility.

In this remodelling, the practice has worked within the tradition of placing a sumptuous, distinctive interior within the restrained historic envelope of a Regency terrace in a way which updates the high-end office environment. The insertion of a characterful atrium, filled with highly crafted artificiality, fills the deep plan with natural light and provides connectivity for the whole house. The restoration in some areas of the house of discrete rooms creates a pleasing dialogue between the traditional hierarchical plan structure and modern flowing space.

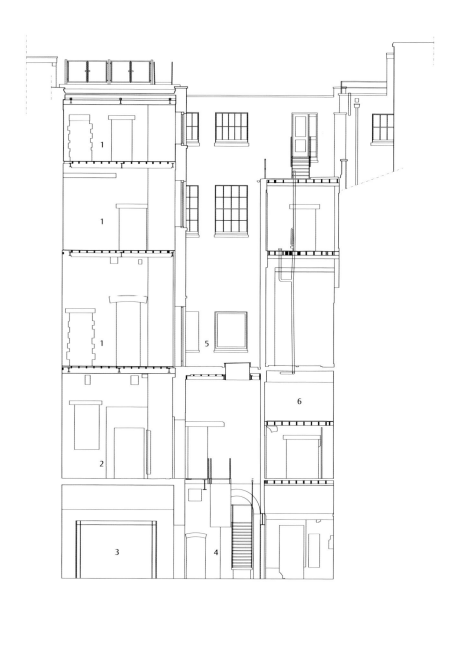

pre-existing section

1 office
2 annex
3 meeting
4 lobby
5 terrace
6 kitchen

0   5m

1:200

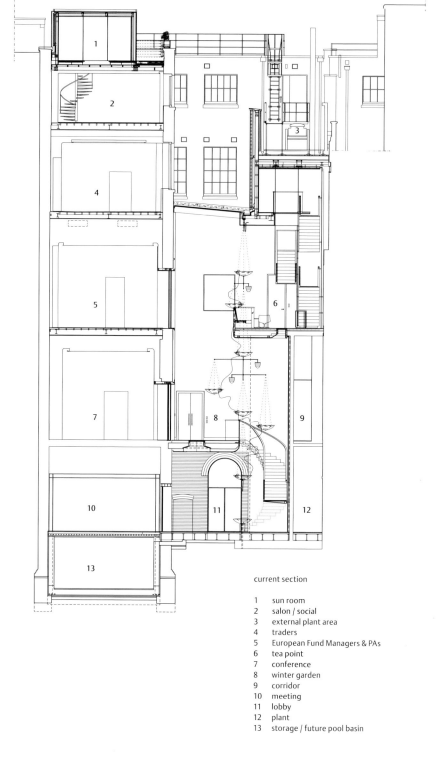

current section

1 sun room
2 salon / social
3 external plant area
4 traders
5 European Fund Managers & PAs
6 tea point
7 conference
8 winter garden
9 corridor
10 meeting
11 lobby
12 plant
13 storage / future pool basin

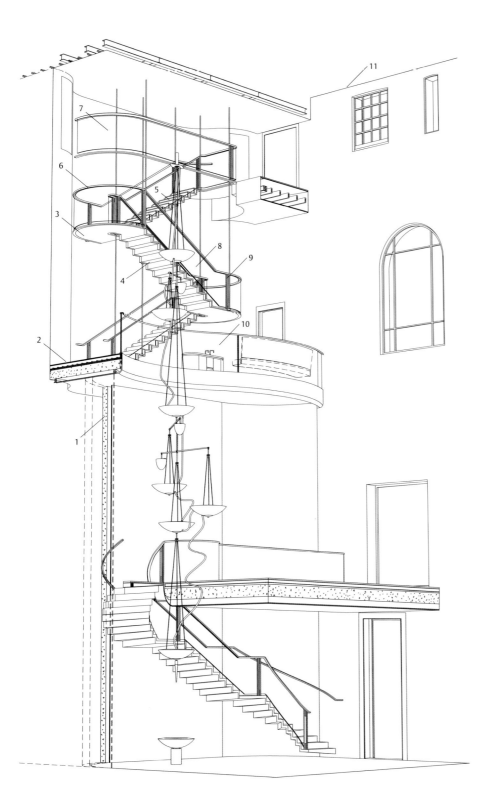

perspectival section and detail

1 concrete wall
2 stone floor
3 stone to stair treads
4 metal cantilevered stair
5 timber treads and risers
6 metal handrail
7 glass balustrade spanning between metal posts
8 cantilevered glass balustrade
9 metal balustrade posts
10 teapoint
11 existing masontry wall

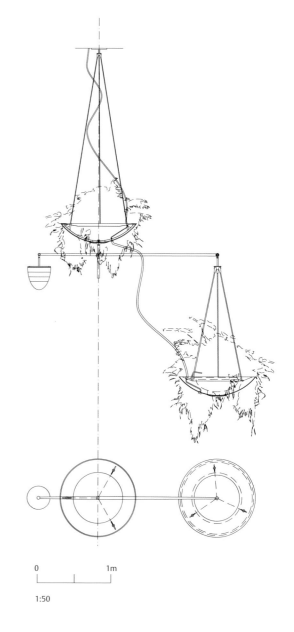

0   1m

1:50

Above: First floor view of the
metal cantilevered stair and the
water fountain.

Right: Ground-floor view of the
winter garden.

London Residence

At Eaton Square, Eric Parry Architects has created a distinctively contemporary home which – while being respectful of the traditional formalities and discretion of the stately Belgravia mansion – also proves to be well suited to informal modern family life. As is often the case in the practice's architecture, the inventive forms and fine, highly crafted materials lend themselves to a metaphorical interpretation. One may perhaps see the layout of the residence in terms of a journey from the more formal rooms facing Eaton Square, down the thematic staircase, to the more primary realm of the family room and finally the garden.

N

0 10 25 50 100m

1:4000

historical sequence
of plans

1   Eaton Square
1*   The King's Road
2   Belgrave Place
2*   Eccleston Street
3   Eaton Place (new)
3*   Eaton Place (old)
4   Eaton Mews (north)
5   Eaton Mews (south)
6   Lyall Street
6*   Elizabeth Street
7   Chester Square
7*   Minerva Street
8   Lowndes Place

1825

1916

In 2013, Eric Parry Architects was commissioned to design a private residence in Eaton Square, one of the grandest squares of the City of Westminster Belgravia Conservation Area. The project, located within a Grade II* listed structure dating from the 1830s, required making a fluid connection between two levels, remodelling all the accommodation and creating a new family room extension with maximum natural light and a close relationship to the private garden at the rear. This is another of the practice's projects for a sumptuous contemporary interior within a protected and discreet neoclassical envelope. An awkward existing relationship with the rear garden has been improved and the residence adapted to contemporary living. The two levels are connected by a feature elliptical stair in the centre of the plan, on axis with the entrance. Recalling the original grand stone cantilevered staircases of London townhouses, it is dramatic in form and highly crafted from stainless steel and terrazzo. It is crowned by a vortex-shaped 'celestial' light sculpture, designed in collaboration with the lighting designer Ingo Maurer. The creation of the family room extension was made possible by the construction of a transfer structure to carry the weight of the rear wall without significant disruption to neighbouring properties. The two levels of the residence are also connected by a highly crafted terrazzo floor, which 'cascades' down the staircase and into the west half of the lower level. The extensively glazed new garden room combines informal dining

with modern family activities. The aim of the remodelling was to re-establish – through contemporary design and the highest quality of materials and craftsmanship – the elegance of the original house.

In 1825 the foremost builder of the time, Thomas Cubitt, agreed with Robert Grosvenor (later the first Marquess of Westminster) to drain and develop the swamp land between London and Chelsea. This area, connecting the town and country, and comprising Belgrave and Eaton Squares and the surrounding streets, became known as Belgravia. Eaton Square was built to the designs of Alexander and Daniel Robertson of 1813. It is a long rectangle – really a widened avenue – containing three pairs of gardens bisected by a thoroughfare, formerly known as The King's Road. Directed towards the new royal residence of Buckingham Palace, its form suggests a ceremonial and processional function, although its gardens were originally leased to market gardeners. The terraces of four or five-storey three-bay stately houses on either side of the square have uniform cream stucco façades, punctuated by giant-order Ionic porticoes, and continuous Doric colonnades surmounted by stucco balustrades. These elements veil the formal reception rooms overlooking the communal gardens. With access bridges over area wells into the side bay of each house, the façades formed a distinctive and dignified entry sequence. These have remained largely unaltered.

above, from left to right: First, plan of urban development surrounding The King's Road (later Eaton Square), based on George Basevi's *Plan of a Leasehold Estate situated at Pimlico in the County of Middlesex belonging to [Earl Grosvenor]* (1825), upon which the new development would receive approval in the House of Commons in 1826; second, modern plan of the development, based on the OS 1916; third, current site plan of Eaton Square by Eric Parry Architects.

right: General view of the typical façades of the urban development around Eaton Square as they stand today.

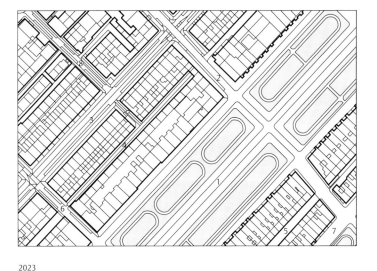

2023

From the early decades of the twentieth century, the use patterns of the houses have undergone substantial changes. As the large single Belgravia mansions became unmanageable following WWI, many were turned to commercial and institutional uses. Eaton Square remained largely residential but lost its exclusive character. The rear elevations between the small gardens and the mews were gradually infilled with a haphazard succession of extensions. In 1952, following bomb damage in WWII, the Grosvenor Estate carried out a major plan to convert the townhouses into lateral flats and maisonettes. This generally involved the removal of two of every three stairs and the creation of communal halls. Only a few apartments retained their own front door. At this time the rear elevations were also substantially reconfigured. The accumulated extensions were removed to allow more light into the flats and to provide the outdoor space required to make the lower ground floor rooms habitable. The demographic and economic changes of recent decades have seen apartments in Eaton Square becoming highly sought after by the wealthy and by international investors, greatly raising land values in the area and setting off a wave of luxury remodelling.

The project's clients were able to renegotiate and consolidate three leases to make up the generous duplex apartment. The work began with the repair of the existing compromised structure and the partial removal of the rear and internal walls. To this end the building above was lifted off its foundations and supported on a transfer slab at upper ground level, with walls around the new staircase and columns to convey the loads to a new ground-floor raft. The structural audacity of this operation recalls Pierre Chareau and Bernard Bijvoet's Maison de Verre in Paris, where the modern new apartment was likewise inserted into an occupied urban block. In this case, however, parts of the internal load-bearing walls were also replaced to create the staircase. It now sits closer to the location of the original 1820s stair, and on axis with the front door. The apartment's front façade thus follows as an A-B-A pattern. This arrangement brings a clear order to the plans, restoring the dignity of the original townhouse.

The entrance from the square is shaded by the colonnade and leads into the long central hall. Without windows to the outside, this space is dramatically illuminated by the light sculpture at the stair end, to which attention is drawn. The hall is flanked by the two reception rooms, full of natural light. Here the practice worked closely with the interior designer Jacques Grange to create relatively formal rooms for the entertaining of guests and the display of the clients' art collection. The door openings were substantially enlarged, producing a sense of contemporary flowing space. To the right of the staircase, an elegant, horsehair-panelled servery and cloak room support entertaining. A passageway to the left,

Eaton Square elevation   1:200

0   5m

which also contains a new lift, leads to a sumptuous master bedroom suite. This occupies the entire back portion of the ground floor. It overlooks a new terrace and the private garden below, which contains a protected, existing magnolia tree. The master bathroom here, as well as the bathrooms downstairs, are fitted out in highly tactile, pale brown travertine, which echoes the nearby finishes of the joinery, horsehair textile and wood flooring. The luxurious detailing deploys large slabs of the stone for the wash basins, wall cladding and cabinetry, so that the bathrooms have minimum visible joints and appear to have been carved out of rock.

The great staircase, encased within a perforated elliptical drum, becomes a key feature around which the residence is oriented. It shares a kinship with the dramatic oval staircases at the Leathersellers' Seventh Hall and the forthcoming 1 Undershaft plaza. Parry likens it to the highly sculptural cantilevered stone and metal staircases of eighteenth and nineteenth-century townhouses. It has an elegant, highly crafted stainless-steel structure, painstakingly fabricated in the workshops of Elite Metalcraft. It is anchored within the fibrous plaster cylinder of the stair hall by stainless steel dowels, so that it does not touch the walls. Lighting around the periphery of the stair emphasises its independence. It is made of welded steel plate and detailed to maximise its sculptural form and sense of vertical movement. The

balustrade, also slightly detached, is held on elliptical-profile posts and made of interlacing steel rods, which give it a delicacy and dynamism. It is topped by a patinated and highly tactile bronze handrail. The curved top landing introduces whiplash curves at floor and handrail level which recall sensual Art Nouveau interiors. These set up a dynamic dialogue with the swirling light sculpture above. Designed by lighting designer Ingo Maurer, this piece amplifies the concavity of the stair hall ceiling. It is made of metal with concealed LED lights strips and is seamlessly integrated into the fibrous plaster drum it illuminates. The slightly convex steps are draped in overlapping prefabricated L-shaped terrazzo panels. These form a seemingly continuous, flowing substance, which melds with the floors at the upper and lower levels. Below the ground-floor landing, the illuminated polished steel plate of the staircase seems to unfold into increasingly gentler angles, in a way which recalls waves touching the shore.

One of the precedents mentioned by Parry in connection with some of the practice's feature stairs are the spectacular free-standing staircases at the centre of many baroque Neapolitan palaces. Centrally located, they are themed as a kind of *axis mundi*, a cosmic structure connecting the luminous celestial realm, the human world, and the elemental depths of earth and water – cave or nymphaeum – where

above: Typical entrance of the development facing Eaton Square, and leading to the ground-floor entrance hall (see p. 66).

left and opposite: The visitor is greeted by the generous space of the library to the left of the hall.

70

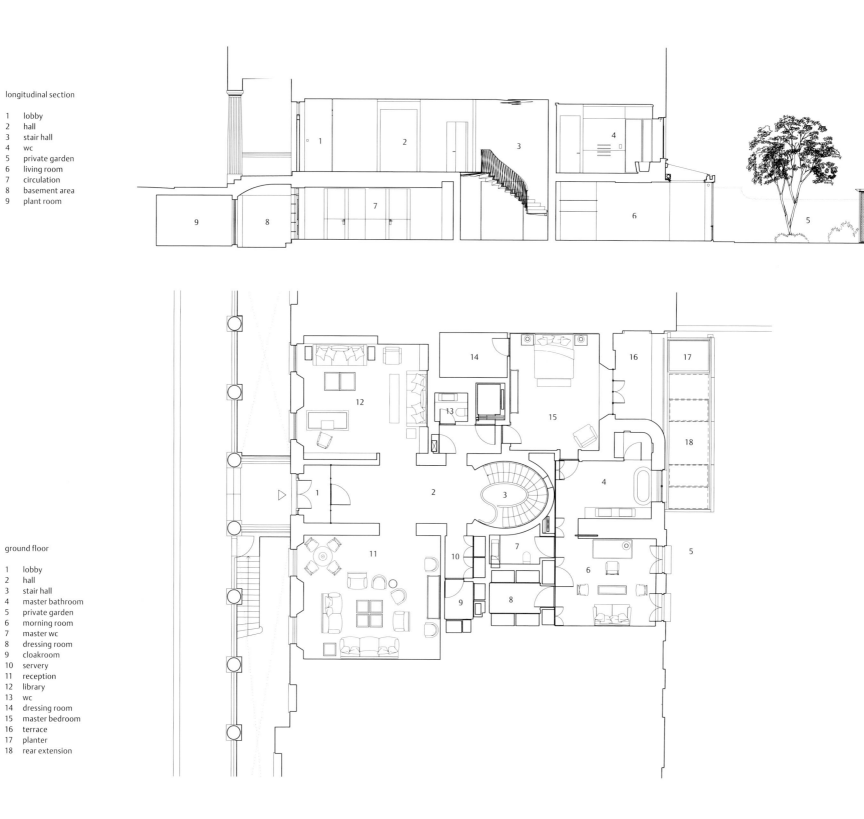

longitudinal section

1 lobby
2 hall
3 stair hall
4 wc
5 private garden
6 living room
7 circulation
8 basement area
9 plant room

ground floor

1   lobby
2   hall
3   stair hall
4   master bathroom
5   private garden
6   morning room
7   master wc
8   dressing room
9   cloakroom
10 servery
11 reception
12 library
13 wc
14 dressing room
15 master bedroom
16 terrace
17 planter
18 rear extension

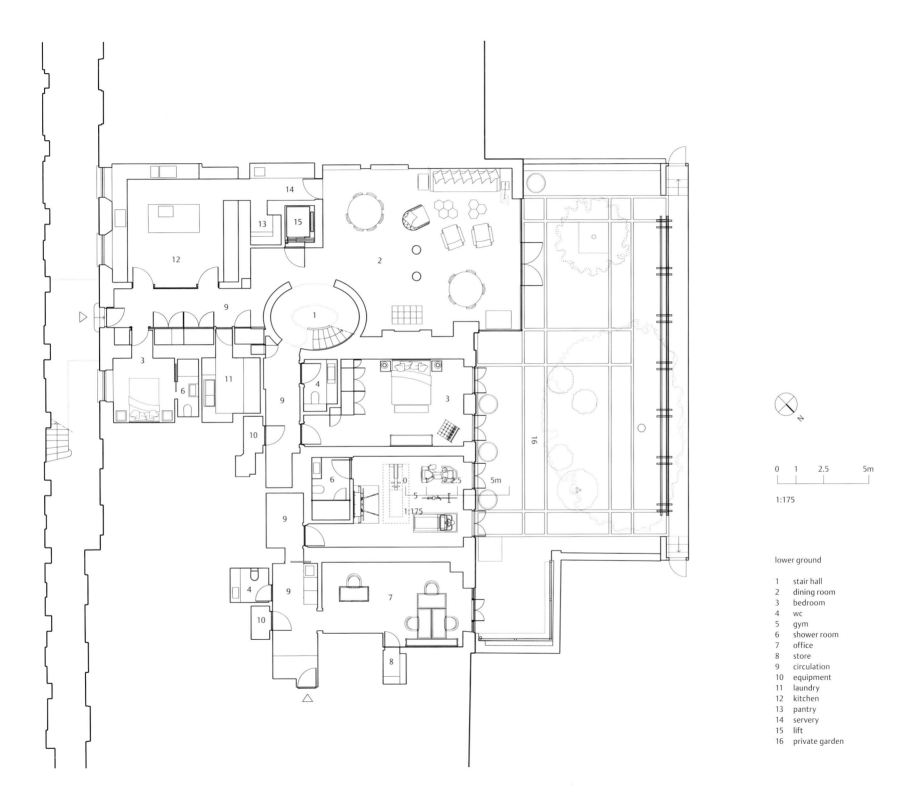

0   1   2.5   5m

1:175

lower ground

1   stair hall
2   dining room
3   bedroom
4   wc
5   gym
6   shower room
7   office
8   store
9   circulation
10   equipment
11   laundry
12   kitchen
13   pantry
14   servery
15   lift
16   private garden

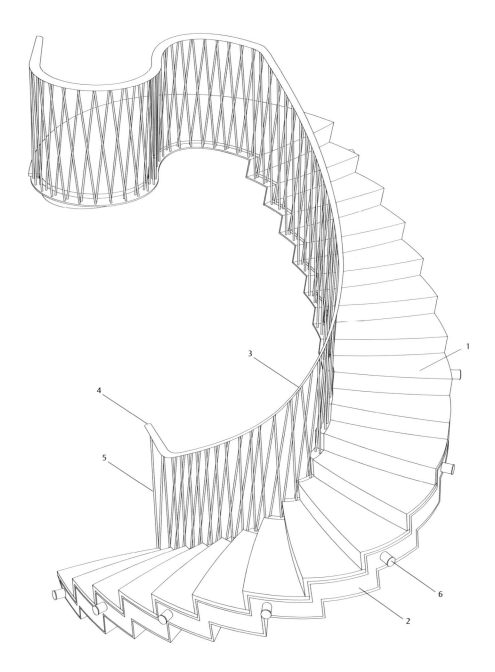

1   precast terrazzo tread with curved edge, and incluned curved riser formed in
    single place and adhered to steel plate
2   decorative metal sofit finish
3   bespoke profile wreath bronze handrail, fixed to steel core rail and balustrade
4   bespoke bronze bullnose end cap to match handrail, fixed to steel core rail
5   12mm balusters fixed to "outrigger" rail, fixed to main stair structure via dowels
6   steel dowels at alternating treads with finish matching adjacent metalwork

opposite, left: Cutaway of the stair at the end of the lobby, leading to the lower ground floor.

opposite, right: Metal structure of the stair.

above: Detail of the balustrade and soffit of the stair.

right: Upward view of the stair hall, culminating in Ingo Maurer's light sculpture.

above: Typical elevation of the back of the development leading to a private terrace.

opposite and right: Views of the dining room on the lower ground overlooking a newly designed private garden.

generative nature is at work. Connecting the controlled world of Eaton Square society with the primordial, wild world of metamorphic stone and verdant nature, this staircase can perhaps be seen in similarly analogical terms.

Parry has great admiration for the 300-year-old Venetian tradition of terrazzo paving. It is a highly crafted material of almost infinite variety, with a wide range of stone aggregates and patterns available. Highly polished, terrazzo can reflect and maximise light. Its durability, sensual qualities and expressive power have often rivalled natural stone in sacred and public buildings or private palaces. Alluding to its metamorphic nature, Parry describes it as "movement in stasis", which brings dynamism to the floor. A petrified liquid, terrazzo is very rich in metaphorical possibilities. For these reasons, it was selected as a means by which to connect the two levels here and to lend thematic content. One of the aims of the design was to create an air of luxury by minimising visible joints between materials, and to form a sense of flow and continuity. To this end, the practice worked with the Vicenza firm of Morseletto, which is known for the high quality of its craftsmanship and illustrious history, having fabricated and supplied pavements, for example, to the buildings of Carlo Scarpa. The terrazzo selected in this case is of a creamy, pale brown hue to maximise the light. It contains two scales of limestone fragments –

finer for the precast stair pieces, and coarser for the poured floors. A natural range of colour shades of limestone in a cream-coloured matrix complements the light browns of the cabinetry, horsehair panelling and travertines used in the apartment. The terrazzo begins on the ground level as a semi-circular collar at the top of the staircase, which traces the form of the stair hall below and reflects the light from above. It changes as it cascades down the curved treads of the staircase. Once it reaches the lower ground level, the terrazzo spreads like lava through the entire western side of the plan, marking a continuity between the stair hall, family room and kitchen. The sensory qualities of the pavement here are crucial; its reflectivity creates a changeable play of light and shadow, and its stone-like hardness speaks of the earth.

The eastern portion of the lower ground accommodation contains a guest room, gym and a self-contained office suite, all with large French doors into the rear garden. The stair hall leads directly into one of the most dramatic components of the residence, the new family room, which mediates between the interior and the garden as a contemporary interpretation of the *sala terrena*. With such a large room, it was important to achieve appropriate proportions, and the slimmer new ground-floor slab granted some half a meter in extra ceiling height. The space here is less structured than

elsewhere, giving rise to inter-related clusters of activity around several key architectural elements: the elliptical stair hall, the dining area set against a wall of display cabinets and linked to the kitchen, intimate seating related to the fireplace, and informal living oriented to the glazed corner and garden. The two massive columns provide subtle demarcation, while also signalling the formidable weight of the building above this earthly region. The full-height gas fireplace in the east wall, clad in hand-made, glossy, greenish ceramic tiles, has a somewhat primal character. The room projects into the garden with large-scale metal-framed glazing and skylight, which flood the terrazzo floor with shimmering, changeable natural light. Internally, the horizontal laylight is a single enormous sheet of translucent glass, which presented a considerable challenge to install and is specially detailed to remain pristine. It subtly defines the garden projection and provides maximum natural light while protecting the room from being overlooked. When viewed from the garden, the glazed corner, with its seemingly granular floor, resembles a giant aquarium. Le Corbusier themed some of the ground level spaces of his celebrated Purist houses, such as the Villa Savoye, as amorphous watery realms, where inhabitants were immersed in verdant nature before ascending to the orthogonally framed spaces of the *piano nobile*. Was Parry thinking of something similar here? If one may read the family garden room metaphorically as a primitive,

subaquatic realm, then its long, uninterrupted laylight recalls the lake's surface. This connects the room to the themes of the spiral staircase.

While the communal gardens of Eaton Square provide civic spaces where the wealthy residents may interact according to social convention, the private rear gardens within the blocks offer an atavistic, restorative escape from the formalities of public life. The landscaping of the garden, designed by Arne Maynard, is based around a highly tactile terracotta pavement. It creates a lush oasis within a dense urban context, with evergreen boundary planting and mews wall screened by trellises of leafy climbers.

At Eaton Square, Eric Parry Architects has created a distinctively contemporary home which – while being respectful of the traditional formalities and discretion of the stately Belgravia mansion – also proves to be well suited to informal modern family life. As is often the case in the practice's architecture, the inventive forms and fine, highly crafted materials lend themselves to a metaphorical interpretation. One may perhaps see the layout of the residence in terms of a journey from the more formal rooms facing Eaton Square, down the thematic staircase, to the more primary realm of the family room and finally the garden.

left: Detail of the horse-hair panelling.

right: View of the dining room from the private garden.

One Chamberlain Square, Paradise Circus, Birmingham

Birmingham was one of the powerhouses of the Industrial Revolution, renowned for bold technical inventiveness and the manufacture of a wide range of products, including chocolate, jewellery, plated metals, textiles and ceramics. Its extensive mercantile activities were facilitated by its infrastructure, most notably its great canal system. The wealth generated by industry, in conjunction with the philosophy of the Midlands Enlightenment, went on to fund much of the civic domain of the city.

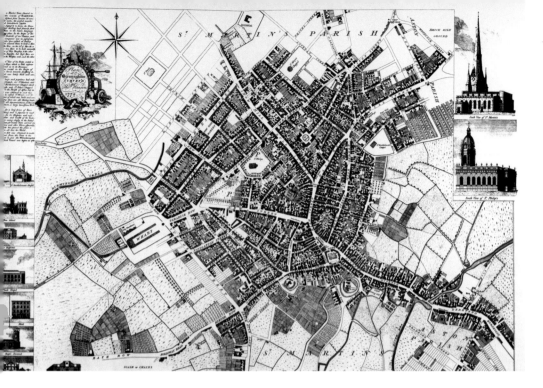

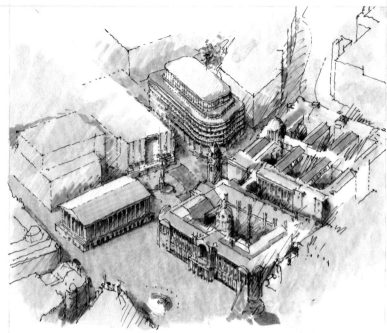

More than perhaps any other British city, Birmingham has seen a dramatic regeneration of its historical core in recent years. The Paradise area had historically been at the heart of the city's civic life. It contains many of its most important nineteenth-century public buildings, including the imposing Grade 1-listed neoclassical Town Hall and the Grade II*-listed Birmingham Museum and Art Gallery. Suffering from economic decline during the second half of the twentieth century, the urban fabric was further damaged by ill-conceived modern planning policies. A new Paradise Masterplan, designed by Glenn Howells Architects for developer Argent and approved in 2013, set out to remedy the city's problems by regenerating the civic character of the area through extensive investment in the quality of the public realm and its buildings, with an emphasis on renewed pedestrian connectivity. After winning an invited competition, Eric Parry Architects was asked to design One Chamberlain Square, a large office block with a commercial base which relates to the surrounding pedestrian domain. The building is at the raised fulcrum of a series of important civic spaces, marking the progression uphill from Victoria to Chamberlain Square and then to the west along Centenary Way to the new Centenary Square, with its commemorative park and ambitious new public library. It will also form a boundary to the new Congreve Square to the northwest, planned in Phase 3. It therefore had to be visually

engaging and approachable from all sides. A decision was made at the outset to respond to the given context here with an organic form, its curvilinear geometry reducing what might otherwise have been an excessive bulk and improving visual connections across the development. The result is a robust building of human scale and rich sensual play of rhythms, hues and surface textures. The gently inflected elevations and rounded corners are enveloped in subtly coloured, glazed-ceramic fins, which give the building a sheen and sense of movement. It follows the classical form of base, body and top, with a setback on the sixth floor forming a perimeter terrace, and another at roof level, which holds the plant. The street views of the building tend to emphasise the cascading curves of its base and cornices. The office storeys and terraces offer remarkable, privileged views of the city and its history.

Birmingham was one of the powerhouses of the Industrial Revolution, renowned for bold technical inventiveness and the manufacture of a wide range of products, including chocolate, jewellery, plated metals, textiles and ceramics. Its extensive mercantile activities were facilitated by its infrastructure, most notably its great canal system. The wealth generated by industry, in conjunction with the philosophy of the Midlands Enlightenment, went on to fund much of the civic domain of the city. It is reflected in its many grand public buildings and cultural

left: Thomas Hanson's *Plan of Birmingham*, surveyed in 1778 (Library of Birmingham).

above: Hand drawing of One Chamberlain Square in the broader urban context of Paradise Circus, by Eric Parry, from July 2014.

One Chamberlain Square
Paradise Circus, Birmingham

Phase 1

1   One Chamberlain Square
2   Two Chamberlain Square
3   Chamberlain Square
4   Paradise Street

Phase 2

5   Three Chamberlain Square
6   Hotel
7   One Centenary Way
8   Centenary Way

Phase 3

9   Two Centenary Way
10 Pavilion
11 Congreve Square
12 One Congreve Square
13 Octagon
14 Three Congreve Square

Other buildings and toponyms

15 Town Hall
16 Birmingham Museum & Art Gallery
17 Council House, Museum and Art Gallery
18 Victoria Square
19 New Street
20 General Post Office
21 Queen's College Chambers
22 Alpha Tower
23 Broad Street
24 Centenary Square
25 Hall of Memory
26 Birmingham Repertory Theatre
27 Library of Birmingham
28 Baskerville House
29 Paradise Circus Queensway
30 Queensway
31 Birmingham Repertory Theatre

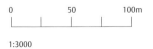

0   50   100m

1:3000

N

Roof plan. Birmingham Paradise Circus option 2 in concrete

Roof plan. Birmingham Paradise Circus option 1 in steel.
10/4/14

ambitions, exemplified in the Paradise area by the Town Hall, Council House, Art Gallery and a sequence of great public libraries. In the late nineteenth century, Birmingham also became one of the centres of the Arts and Crafts movement, and especially of ceramic production. Having emerged alongside and as a consequence of industrialisation, this craft was nurtured at the new Birmingham Municipal School of Art. The innovative Ruskin Pottery company was highly influential and is strongly represented in the Birmingham Museum and Art Gallery.

Despite considerable bomb damage incurred during the Blitz, the city's economy remained strong during the 1950s and '60s. At this time, its optimism and civic pride manifested themselves in the City Council's enthusiastic adoption of the scientistic principles of modern planning, allowing, for example, traffic engineering to dominate urban redevelopment to the detriment of pedestrian life. A new civic centre was planned for the Paradise, of which John Madin's Brutalist library was the only fully realised fragment. The development was marred by the carving up of the area by a ring of motorways, and by the separation of functions and levels, which made it dank and impenetrable. In recent decades, Birmingham has become a thriving centre of the service, communications and financial industries. Despite the continuing deprivation of some of its areas, the city has seen much success at reinventing itself. The new Paradise Masterplan

is part of this effort to rebuild dignity and civic spirit by improving the public realm for people. Its ultimate success remains to be seen, but the outlook is hopeful.

The Chamberlain Square site rises steeply from the Town Hall towards the north west, and is focused on a large Victorian public fountain, a handsome civic amenity and a memorial to the businessman and politician after whom the square is named. The architecture of the Town Hall was based on a Roman temple and intended perhaps to bring to mind the republican virtues of the Forum Romanum. Built in the 1830s, it was the first of the monumental town halls to grace the prosperous cities of Victorian England and was always used for public assemblies and cultural events. The square resembles a natural amphitheatre, and has been landscaped as such, with broad stone steps for people to sit and to participate in the drama of civic life.

The new One Chamberlain Square has a concrete frame structure and a roughly trapezoidal plan, with curved corners and subtle inflections on the south and east elevations. The geometry of the envelope, seen from different viewpoints, creates visual variety. The tall ground floor is at the level of the pavement and very much grounded in the pedestrian domain of the area. An early Parry sketch of the building shows the base as an open colonnade, recalling the multi-purpose

above: Early hand drawing by Eric Parry, dating from 10 April 2014, for One Chamberlain Square, showing an undulating steel structure as the first option.

left: Hand drawing by Eric Parry, showing a rectangular, round-cornered concrete structure as a second option.

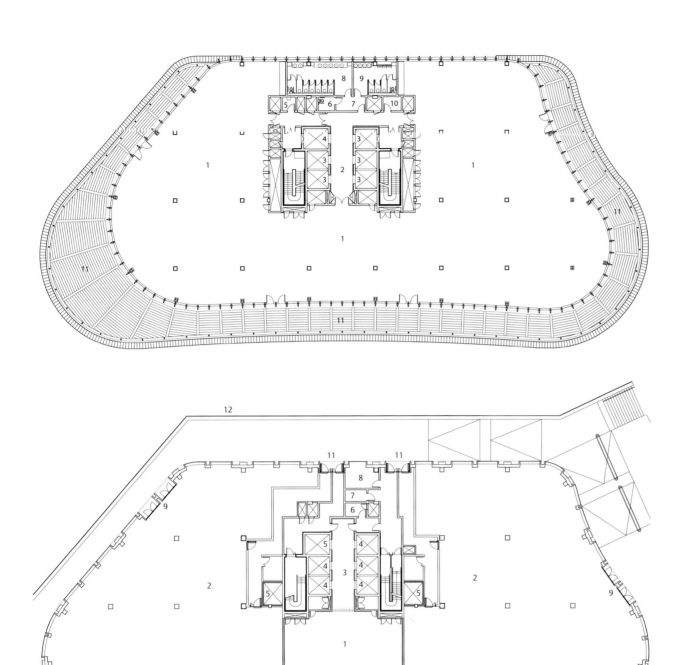

6th floor plan

1. office
2. lift lobby
3. passenger lift
4. goods lift
5. cleaners' cupboard
6. accessible wc
7. wc lobby
8. female wc
9. male wc
10. store
11. terrace

ground floor plan

1. office lobby
2. retail
3. lift lobby
4. passenger lift
5. goods lift
6. FM/BMS
7. accessible wc
8. fire control room
9. retail entrance
10. office entrance
11. fire exit
12. edge of Phase 1 podium

0   10m

1:500

N

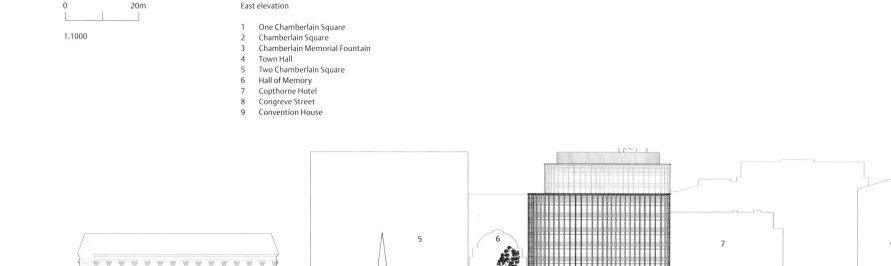

0   20m

1:1000

East elevation

1   One Chamberlain Square
2   Chamberlain Square
3   Chamberlain Memorial Fountain
4   Town Hall
5   Two Chamberlain Square
6   Hall of Memory
7   Copthorne Hotel
8   Congreve Street
9   Convention House

secular buildings of the agora or forum. The masterplan has provided robust stone landscaping with outdoor dining areas, seating and colourful planting. The ground level piers and lintels are encased in dark grey, polished precast concrete with exposed aggregate. Most of the retail glazing takes the form of elegant individual oriel windows and doorways in bronze-finish frames, which give the façade depth. The entrance to the office reception lobby is off Centenary Way. This long elevation is very slightly concave, giving the south-facing pavement a more generous dimension. The entry itself is formed by great receding curved-glass panels. The large lobby leads to the service core. This central section of the plan is flanked by retail units with street access from the south, east and west. These contain chiefly restaurants and cafés, an important component of the street life here.

The floor-to-ceiling glazing of the curvilinear body of the building allows natural light to reach deep into the office floor plates. The core, located at the northern side of the building, has finely crafted finishes and understated detailing. Toilets are located behind the north elevation and also receive abundant daylight, a feature much enjoyed by the building's occupants. The skin of the façade steps back at the sixth floor, creating a terrace around its periphery, and again at the top, where it reduces the visual impact of the roof plant. The flexible office space has been fitted out by the primary tenant.

Work areas are mostly arranged in loose clusters around transparent-wall meeting rooms, with no corridors. The majority of workers thus experience a pleasing sense of openness and light. The panoramic views from the upper floors are breathtaking, revealing many familiar Birmingham landmarks anew and in startling proximity.

The apparently organic, curved and subtly inflected shape of the building was developed in the earliest stages of design. It mitigates what would otherwise have been the impact of a very large rectangular mass, and creates continuity around the corners. Equally importantly, the building's flowing geometry is the source of its particular architectural character, giving it a certain voluptuousness. When seen from different viewpoints, the curves of the base lintel line and of the two cornices appear as serpentine lines which seem to flex and undulate relative to each other. Parry likes this sense of implicit movement, noting it as one of the key aesthetic principles described by William Hogarth in his book *The Analysis of Beauty* (1753). Due to its siting, the large-radius curve of the southeast corner 'noses' forward. It becomes in effect the building's chief façade, presiding over Chamberlain Square. The external envelope, consisting of aluminium curtain wall and ceramic-clad ribs, is similar to that deployed at Fen Court. The curvilinear geometry here, however, creates quite different impacts.

above: Eastward view from
Centenary Square, with
One Chamberlain Square
in the distance; on the left,
Baskerville House; on the right,
the Hall of Memory.

right: Westward view alongside
One Chamberlain Square.

South elevation

1 One Chamberlain Square
2 Centenary Way
3 Chamberlain Square
4 Copthorne Hotel
5 Convention House
6 Birmingham Museum & Art Gallery
7 Birmingham Museum & Art Gallery Bridge
8 Paradise Circus Queensway
9 Queensway

0   20m

1:1000

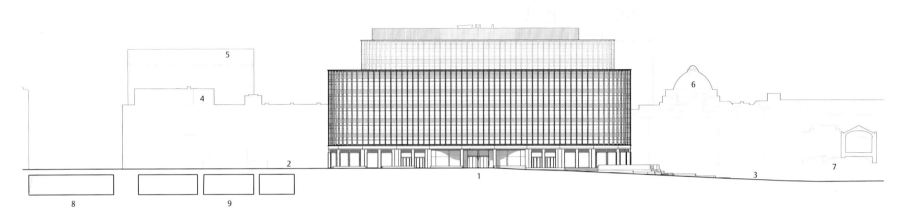

left: Arriving from Victoria Square, a view of One Chamberlain Square photographed in August 2022 during the Commonwealth Games; on the left: the Corinthian order of the Town Hall and the spire of the Chamberlain Memorial Fountain; on the right: the corner of the Council House, Museum and Art Gallery.

Very important in the overall effect is the way in which the curves play with the verticals, creating changing rhythms and surface textures. The sense of curvilinear movement is accentuated by the building's ceramic-clad envelope. It was created through an interaction between the glazing system and a veil of ceramic-clad vertical ribs, which link and to some extent conceal the necessary faceting of the façade. Only the ground-floor lintels and glazing, and the typical level *brise-soleil* have a slight curvature. The overall sense of curvilinearity is created through the use of predominantly straight components. The aluminium curtain wall system used here is a grid of prefabricated floor-to-ceiling glazing units at 1.5m centres. These are connected on the outside by gaskets which allow a slight flexibility in the relationship between the units, thus absorbing the elevations' subtle curvatures. The ceramic cladding of the projecting ribs consists of three extruded sections: a nose at the front and two angled cheek panels. These ribs give the elevation a depth and some protection from solar gain. The ceramic creates the constantly changing textures of reflections and colours, which harmonise with the mellow stones of the nearby public buildings. Horizontally, the elevation is modulated by opaque glass spandrel panels and floor-to-ceiling glazing. The glass is treated up to desktop level with 50% frit, a pattern digitally imprinted on the inner surface of the double-glazing panels. This is a chemical process, linking the manufacture of glass with that of glazed ceramics, and alludes to their implicit affinities. In this case, the

mottled, semi-opaque pattern of the lower window section – a kind of dado – provides a degree of privacy, while giving the full-height glazing a sense of human scale. The frit pattern also creates visual echoes with the colour and texture of the ceramic cladding of the ribs.

The horizontal rhythm of the office floors is further enriched by rows of aluminium *brise-soleil*. As at Fen Court, these are treated with a polychromatic metal paint, so that in addition to controlling solar gain, they bring subtle, changeable hues – ranging from green and orange to purple – to the composition. One can best appreciate the colour and texture modulations at close range, as for example on the terrace, where the mottled, glossy and variable surface of the ceramic ribs (resting on a darker grey, precast concrete foot) interacts with the frit texture of the window 'dado', and the colourful accents of the *brise-soleil*. The fabric of sensual resonances is further expanded by the texture of the white river pebbles at the base of the windows and the granite terrace paving slabs. Viewed from street level, the convex and concave curved surfaces of the building's elevations appear to be variably light and dark, open and closed, immaterial and solid.

Parry's deployment of subtly modulated ceramic cladding can be seen here as a reference to the Arts and Crafts pottery once cultivated in the city and displayed in the Art Gallery next door. Ruskin Pottery

The visual dynamism of the undulating façade promotes a continuous dialogue with the urban kinetics of the square, here seen in two aspects of what could be described as a visual dance.

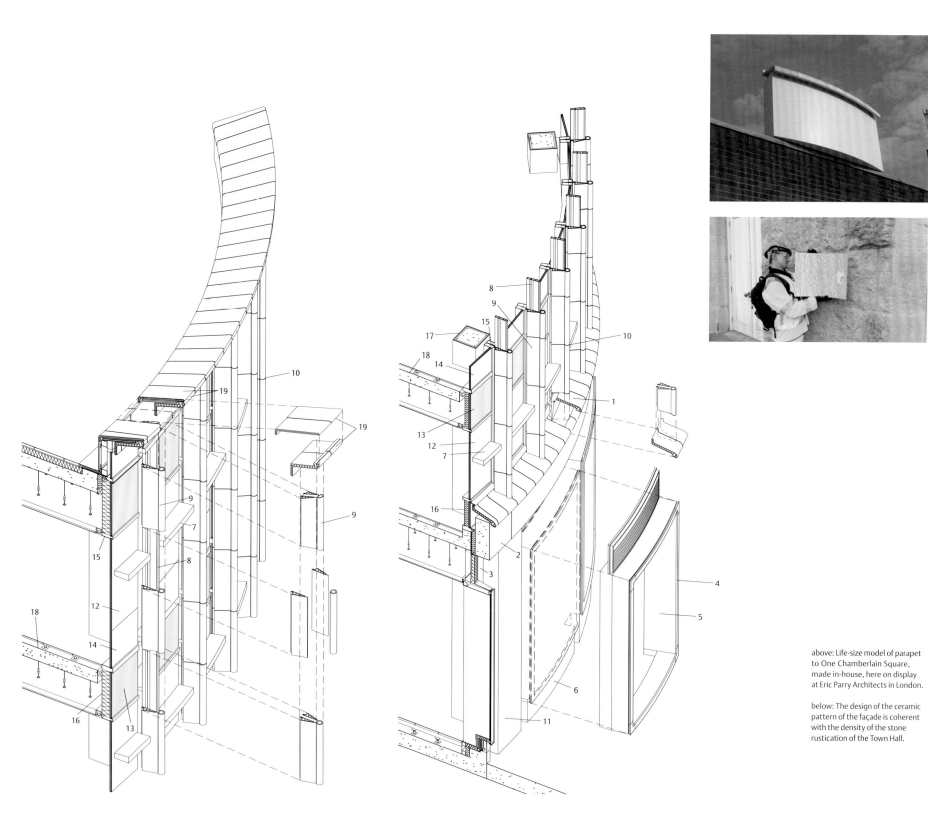

above: Life-size model of parapet to One Chamberlain Square, made in-house, here on display at Eric Parry Architects in London.

below: The design of the ceramic pattern of the façade is coherent with the density of the stone rustication of the Town Hall.

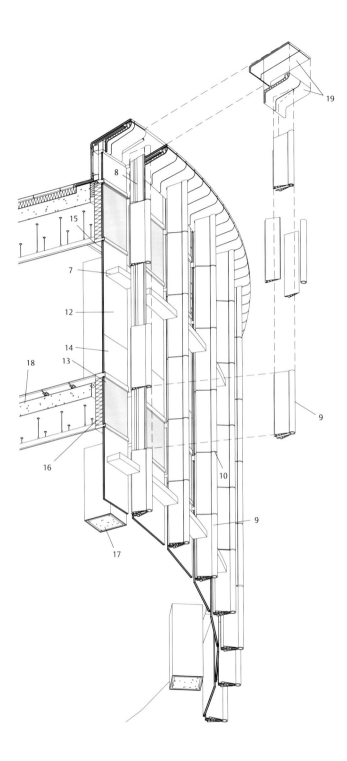

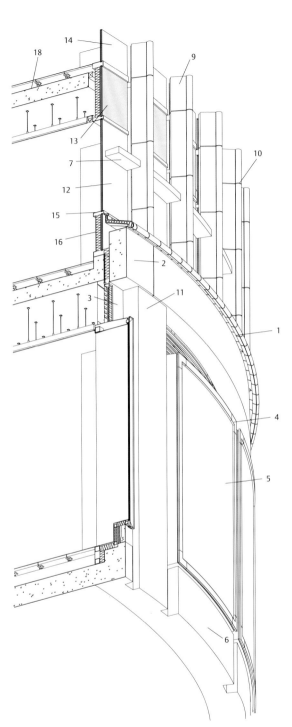

perspectival section

1 terracotta cill with two-coloured, twice-fired glaze
2 polished precast concrete lintel
3 3mm thick profiled aluminium shopfront surrounds
4 3mm thick capping fixed to shopfront window frame, bronze metal antique finish
5 shopfront glazing, laminated low iron safety glass
6 80mm thick polished precast concrete skirt to base of retail shop front
7 aluminium brise-soleil (straight / curved on corner units) with Qualicoat Class 2 PPC dichroic colour paint, fixed back to curtain walling system
8 stainless steel bracketry to support vertical terracotta fin
9 vertical terracotta fin with two-coloured, twice-fired glaze
10 10mm open joint
11 polished precast concrete pier with exposed aggregate on all visible surfaces
12 clear double-glazed unit
13 glazed spandrel panel with 100% frit to inner pane
14 50% frit to glazing up to 800 from FFL
15 aluminium curtain walling system with Qualicoat Class 2 PPC finish. System providing lateral support for vertical terracotta fins
16 rock wool insulation behind spandrel panel
17 encased structural concrete columns
18 concrete slab
19 terracotta cornice and coping with two-coloured, twice-fired glaze

was famous particularly for its highly sensual glazes: misty glazes which mimicked the effects of ice crystals, lustre glazes which recalled metallic finishes, and visceral flambé glazes which evoked pools of blood. These daily objects were thus also expressions of the metaphorical qualities – the myriad connections between things – which animate the experiential world. The chemical formulations for the Ruskin glazes were able to transform the base matter of clay into something noble and were closely guarded. An admiration for this tradition is evident here.

Finally, one may remark on Eric Parry Architects' approach to the order of the urban sphere here. All the historical public buildings facing Chamberlain Square do so with classical orders. This is also the case for the new office building across the street at 2 Chamberlain Square, where the entire main façade assumes the form of an attenuated, abstracted classical portico. This is an understandable reaction, perhaps, given the Town Hall's temple-like form and allusions to the Roman Forum. Parry's approach is different, however. One is tempted to see his restrained response and choice of references as an implicit recognition of a certain idea

of civic decorum, a view which implies that there is an appropriate architectural expression for different categories of buildings. Instead of aiming for another conspicuous building (which an allusion to a classical portico would represent) his architecture seems rather to aspire to be an integral part of the urban fabric, where it would hold its own. As he said, the building's aim is to act as a backdrop to the civic architecture of the square. There are good reasons for this, chief among them being a respect for the tradition of a coherent urban hierarchy. In other words, in the situational setting of the town centre, urban texture (or *poché*) is as important as the iconic public buildings to which it creates a foil. Part of this civilised tradition has been a recognition that institutions of collective and civic significance – government, justice, religion, education and so forth – merit a more honorific form of expression, and that private buildings, which provide a setting for work but lack such a public import, best remain relatively low key. Their chief responsibility, in addition to providing a good work environment for their occupants, is to contribute to forming a legible urban order. This principle, which is often ignored in today's image-driven architecture, is worth upholding.

left: Façade of One Chamberlain Square during installation of the terracotta fins to the fifth floor.

above: Detail of the base of a terracotta fin to the setback volume, rising from the sixth floor terrace.

right: View of the setback, generating two voices or melodic lines to the undulating façade.

Wilmar Headquarters, Singapore

The plaza, which receives sunlight through an 8-shaped oculus, contains the entrances to the main office reception, an exhibition space and a café. Above, the building resembles an assemblage of curvilinear trays, stepping back with each successive level on the park side to create garden terraces. As a result, all workspace has a direct connection to verdant landscape, making it more pleasant and stimulating.

After winning an invited international design competition in Singapore in 2017, Eric Parry Architects was commissioned to design the landmark headquarters for the agribusiness group Wilmar International. The building is situated in the new Biopolis science park in the eastern portion of the city. This area had been part of a Zaha Hadid Architects' masterplan, which sought to create a lively, mixed-use and pedestrian-friendly new precinct. The practice's chief aim was to design a distinctive and sustainable building, which would actively interact with the local context of tropical climate (hot and humid alternating with hot and wet) and undulating topography of urban parks. The building, realised in collaboration with the local architectural firm RSP Architects, is a seven-storey structure of organic form, with tiered landscape terraces overlooking the adjoining public park. The shaded double-height entry plaza contains four pairs of giant steel-encased columns. Expertly fabricated and finished, these are reminiscent of mature trees, and carry uplighters which illuminate the shimmering ceramic soffit. The plaza, which receives sunlight through an 8-shaped oculus, contains the entrances to the main office reception, an exhibition space and a café. Above, the building resembles an assemblage of curvilinear trays, stepping back with each successive level on the park side to create garden terraces. As a result, all workspace has a direct connection to verdant landscape, making it more pleasant and stimulating. With his fondness for the expressive architectural simile, Parry likens this form to a pile of stacked crockery, though it has locally been seen as referencing Asian rice terraces. The two cores rise up through differently shaped wings. The north wing, which contains the exhibition space and café, is enclosed in distinctive, 'open-weave' diamond-shaped glazing, which maximises a sense of openness. In addition to the grand hall of the office reception, the south wing contains an auditorium and meeting rooms, encased within an opaque, somewhat bulbous form with deep-slit windows. This volume is clad in curved natural anodised aluminium panels to amplify its sculptural form. The laboratory and office floors above have ribbons of glazing which provide 360-degree views, and horizontal ceramic-clad fins designed to shade and cool the building and to cast off rainwater. The building's biophilic elements contribute to the well-being of its occupants and also provide a habitat for a diverse range of tropical flora and fauna.

An affluent global city, Singapore has been promoting itself as an attractive place for companies looking to expand their presence in Asia. With its excellent infrastructure and capable workforce, it has attracted many international companies, including Dyson, Google and UBS. In a competitive labour market, providing high-

left: View of Wilmar Headquarters during construction in January 2020.

right: Bird's-eye view from July 2021 of the completed building.

site plan

1   main reception
2   auditorium
3   exhibition space
4   café
5   meeting spaces
6   northern entrance
7   bicycle and BOH entrance
8   One-North link
9   Biopolis Road
10 Portsdown Road
11 Central Exchange Green

0   20m

1:1000

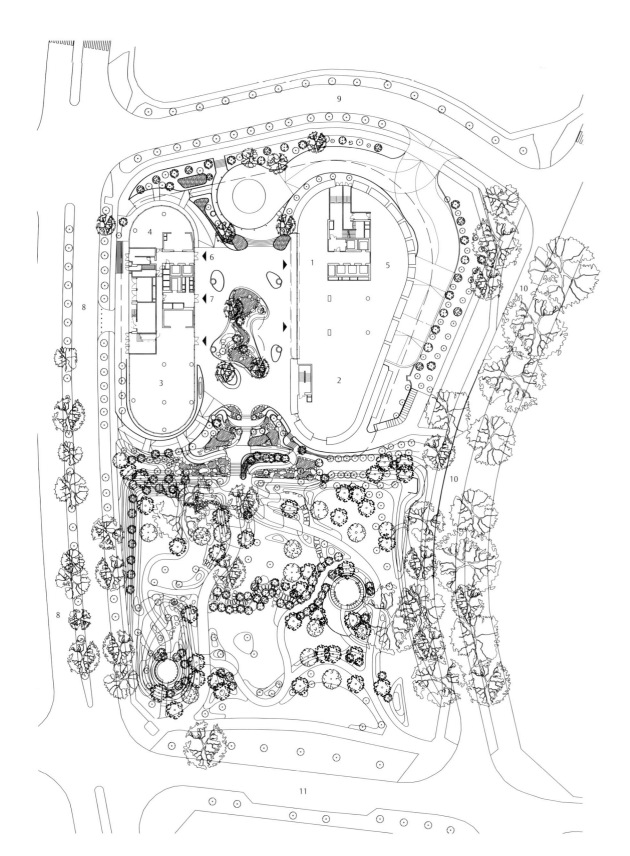

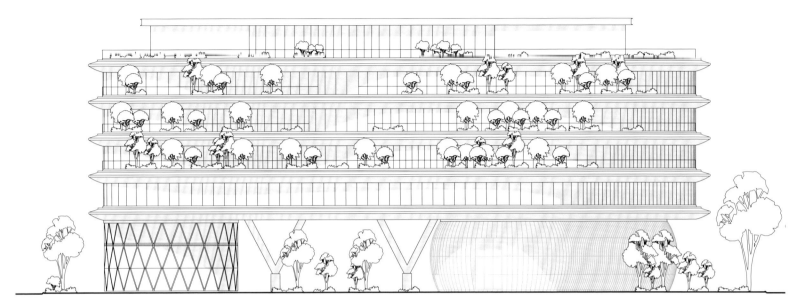

west elevation

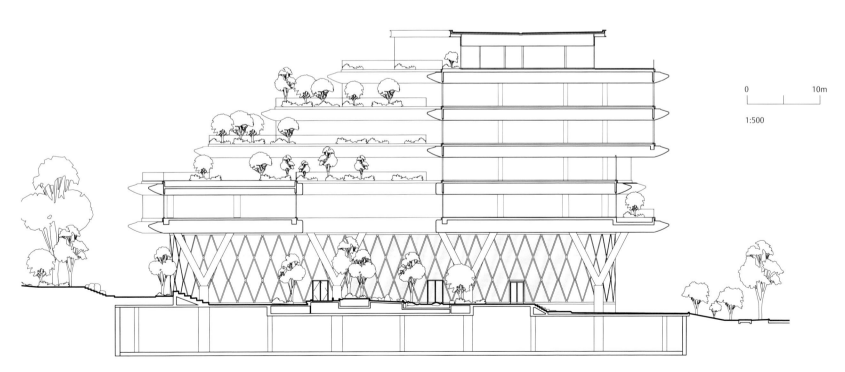

section

0   10m

1:500

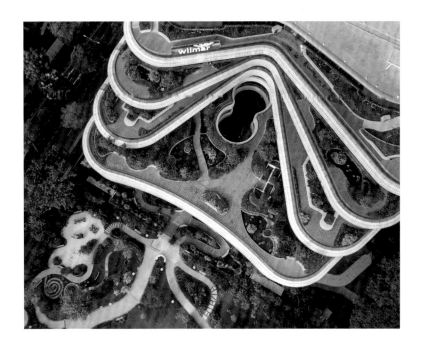

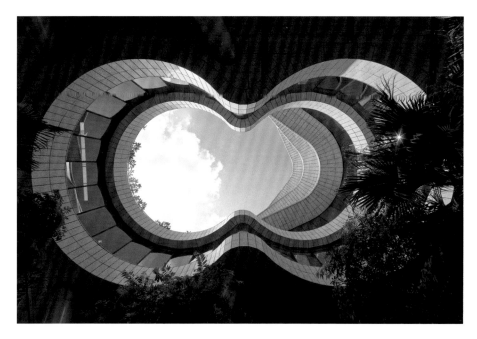

left: View of the double-height space of the entry plaza. The ceramic soffit upper floor (level 3) is supported by eight giant tree-like steel-encased concrete columns with four-way branches, and punctuated by the figure-8 of a large oculus, which allows in natural light.

above: Downward view of the receding landscaped setbacks that shelter the entrance of natural light into the arrival plaza below through the figure-8 oculus.

right: Upward view of the oculus, framing the sky, inhabited by the adjoining receding levels 3 to 7.

quality, enjoyable workspace has become a way of attracting and retaining staff. The recent One-North masterplan by Zaha Hadid Architects has been created with these things in mind. It set out to redefine the typical bland, industrial park of disconnected buildings. The masterplan vision, yet to be fully realised, was to create a characterful, inclusive and pedestrian-friendly environment, mixing work, educational, recreational and residential uses in a Green City setting. The site is unusual in the development, in that the parcel of land is an island, open on all sides. The building form mediates the transition between workspace and park.

The entry plaza at the base of the building is a large, double-height, publicly accessible realm of civic ambitions. It is like a vessel of cooling shadow, which at times is pierced by a dramatic shaft of sunlight coming through the figure-8 oculus. It contains lush landscaping with biodiverse planting and curvilinear basins, which receive a natural internal waterfall pouring from the oculus during the frequent tropical downpours. The most notable feature here are the eight giant steel-encased concrete columns. With four-way branches, they cluster the structure to keep the space below uncluttered. They resemble muscular trees, lifting up the ceramic soffit above the plaza like a forest canopy. Something of an engineering marvel, their 20mm thick steel tubes are welded together to form permanent shuttering for

the concrete and its reinforcements. Their challenging construction involved continuous two-day welding sessions, followed by intense finishing to achieve the perfectly smooth painted surface. In addition to their biomorphic connotations, the giant tree-columns are something of a homage to the local highly skilled marine industry. The soffit, a full 10.5m above the granite pavement, is clad in ceramic panels which reflect light and complement the colour of the columns. The oculus is likewise lined in ceramic. One of the important requirements of building in a tropical climate is the creation of shade and cross breezes, and the plaza provides a pleasant, naturally cool setting. Most of the workforce arrive into it by a public walkway which is linked with the drop-off at the east side. The somewhat hierarchical local tradition has required a separate drop-off and lift lobby for the owners, and these lead to their penthouse offices. Parking, extensive bicycle facilities and services are on the lower ground level.

Above the plaza, the building consists of curvilinear floor plates, each receding further back on the west side, allowing light into the oculus. This creates break-out terraces for the laboratory and office levels. These are elaborately landscaped with curvaceous planters and water features, and alive with colourful flowers and butterflies. They provide views of the park through glass balustrades. With a relatively deep office plan, the ceiling heights are generous, almost double

level 6

1 core
2 wc
3 office
4 terrace

level 7

1 core
2 office
3 terrace

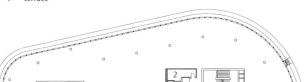

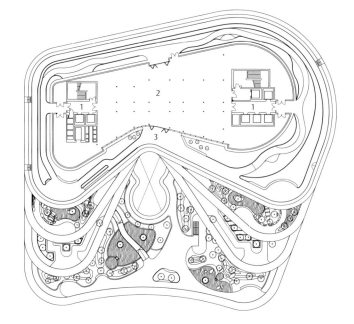

0   20m

1:1000

level 3

1 core
2 wc
3 laboratory
4 terrace

level 5

1 core
2 wc
3 office
4 terrace

opposite: View of the ground
level by the end of the dry season

height. The envelope comprises ribbon glazing to maximise views. Below this, continuous 2m-wide ceramic-clad fins act as awnings to provide solar shading to the glazing. The extruded ceramic cladding is a stable and durable material, its shimmering glaze responding to changing light conditions. A base grey colour is speckled with white, which gives the glaze a tactile texture and a sense of depth. The ceramic panels of the fins are attached to an overhanging steel structure. A bullnose detail on the lip ensures that torrential water is cast off, to be collected below. The fins provide a large part of the building's architectural interest, creating a constantly shifting topography when seen from different directions. They also resonate with the organic forms of the landscaping and provide walkways protected from rain and sun. As at One Chamberlain Square, the building's curvilinear envelope was created entirely using orthogonal components, which greatly reduced costs.

The two ground-level wings, on which the curvilinear office trays appear to rest, were part of the initial diagrammatic idea. The convex wing encasing the south core appears to be a pneumatic cushion, compressed by the weight of the building. This biomorphic 'pebble' contains an auditorium and a series of break-out meeting rooms with deep slit windows. After considering the use of highly reflective stainless steel, the architects decided on matt anodised aluminium

cladding to minimise any glare to neighbouring buildings. It gives the back of this volume a sense of mystery, while the broad glazing of the main office reception hall after dusk fills the plaza with a warm glow. The north wing is an elongated glass cylinder wrapped in a translucent weave and resembling the mesh basket on old soda bottles. It houses publicly accessible facilities: an exhibition space and café, surmounted at level 2 by office space to be leased to start-ups. Open all day, these ensure the building and its plaza retain a sense of civic life. The architects' verbal imagery hints at the analogical thinking behind the design.

On the interior the practice were responsible for the design of the lift cars and lift lobbies. The walls of the lift lobbies are clad in thick panels of travertine, a highly tactile material ranging in colour here between soft beige and chocolate. These are laid vertically, in sections separated by upright metal reveals in bronze-coloured anodised aluminium to maximise the sense of height. The floors are paved in cream-coloured book-matched slabs of Colorado Gold Vein marble, which is cream-coloured with subtle golden-brown veining. The metal lift door frames are also of an aureate hue. The tall lift lobbies are enclosed by glazed fire doors and aligned in such a way as to allow views across the two cores to the daylight on the other side. It was considered important, given the depth of the plan, to provide points of orientation to the outside which would make the workspace

left: View of one of the tree-like column shafts before transportation onto the construction site.

above: Life-size model of the ground-level façade of the exhibition space and café.

opposite: Life-size model for the upper levels of the façade.

axonometric detail

1   insulated glass unit with solar coated interlayer
2   curved aluminium flashing with integrated mansafe system
3   stainless steel maintenance walkway with integrated lighting
4   glazed ceramic brise-soleil fixed to galvanised steel subframe
5   aluminium blind box
6   suspended plasterboard ceiling
7   post tension concrete slab
8   raised floor system

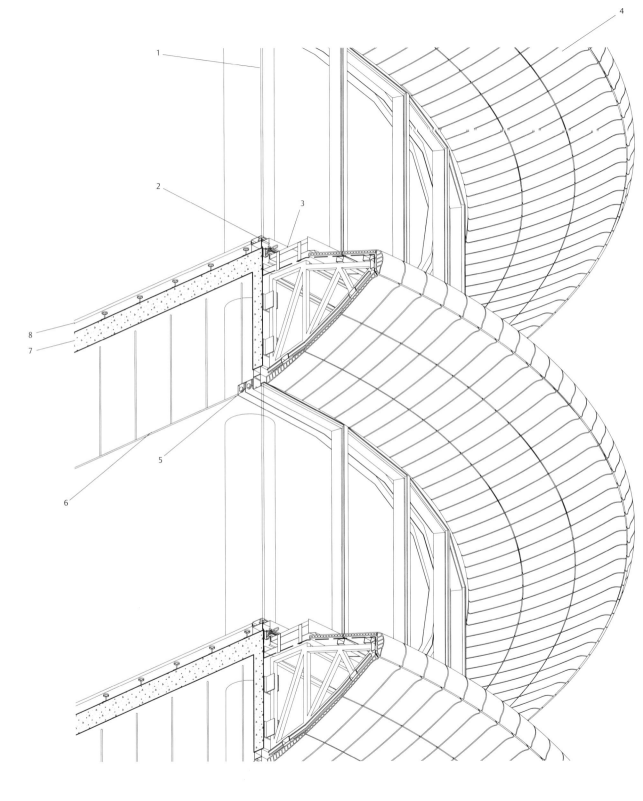

more navigable and pleasant. The interior finishes and lighting were selected to produce a warm, luxurious glow, subtly suggestive of gold, a material considered propitious in the local culture. The warm tones contrast agreeably with the cool colour palette of the glazing, steel and ceramic cladding of the exterior. The clients' fit-out included a curved staircase between the office levels, reducing the dependence on lifts.

Singapore's heavy rainfall has led to the use of covered walkways around buildings to protect pedestrians from intense sun and rain. The present design interprets this custom by having walkways around its periphery, which are sheltered by the overhanging ceramic fins of the office floors. There are also covered walkways which lead arrivals from the park into the plaza, making movement around and under the building – surrounded by colourful biodiverse planting – an enjoyable experience.

In a new precinct where there is not much historical context, Eric Parry Architects' sensitive and inventive design has taken its architectural cues from the characteristics of the natural setting, namely the tropical climate and lush vegetation of Singapore. It creates a high-quality work environment by manipulating natural shade and cooling, and by harnessing the heavy rainfall and panoramic views to architectural ends. It also responds to certain local customs, such as the hierarchical arrangement of the entries or the traditional veneration of gold. In providing a good, sustainable place to work, it satisfies the place-making aspirations outlined in the masterplan, and suggests a fruitful strategy of future tropical office architecture.

left: Eas
levels v
ground

right: S
the upp
tree-lik
pebble-
receptio
the bac

opposit
projecti
levels 3
sets bac
structu
landsca
with the

Vicarage Gate House, London

The chief feature of the new block are the different ways in which its façades balance vertical and horizontal elements so as to echo the traditional scale and rhythm of the street, while also producing a dynamic contemporary feel. The historical site area provides a rich setting. To the east, it is bounded by the exclusive private road of Kensington Palace Gardens, lined by late nineteenth-century stucco or brick mansions, standing behind security fences and enveloped in private gardens.

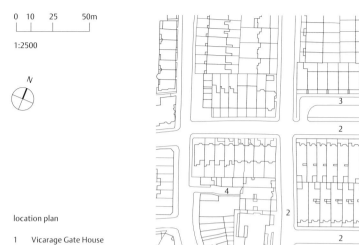

N

location plan

1 Vicarage Gate House
2 Vicarage Gate
3 Inverness Gardens
4 Melon Place
5 Kensington Palace Gardens

Vicarage Gate House occupies a prominent corner site at the junction of Vicarage Gate and Palace Gardens Terrace in South Kensington, a stone's throw from Kensington Palace. The brief was to create a sophisticated residential development of 14 apartments that would complement the existing residences in the heart of the Kensington Conservation Area, whilst providing a benchmark for quality design. The form of the building is devised to suggest a mixture of multi-level town houses – typical of this area and continuing the street façade – and modern lateral apartments. Its main entrance is from Vicarage Gate, with a generous landscaped courtyard to the rear. The adroit design of the section enabled an insertion in the lower half of the building of an extra level, while maintaining the street cornice lines and generous ceiling heights within. The practice is known for their ability to create imaginative, daylit subterranean spaces and that skill is deployed here. The lower ground level accommodates residential units arranged around elegant lightwell courtyards and a sky-lit residents' gym over basement service areas and parking. The building massing and façade design are highly responsive to the existing context. The north elevation complements the existing neighbouring terrace on Vicarage Gate, with traditional masonry brickwork, bay windows framed in polished cream precast concrete, and smaller recessed windows above. The top level comprises elegant penthouse accommodation within a zinc mansard roof, surrounded by perimeter

terraces. A ceramic-clad bay with curved windows, which projects from the east side of the front elevation, celebrates the complexity of the building's location. To the east, a stepped terrace arrangement provides residents with generous external living spaces. The south elevation consists of brick piers and vertical panels of full-height picture windows, traversed by horizontal bands of precast. There are seven large balconies which offer private amenity space to each of the apartments. Internally, the units are generously proportioned and planned for ease of living, with the primary spaces generally oriented to the world of gardens to the south and east. The chief feature of the new block is the different ways in which its façades balance vertical and horizontal elements so as to echo the traditional scale and rhythm of the street, while also producing a dynamic contemporary feel.

The historical site area provides a rich setting. To the east, it is bounded by the exclusive private road of Kensington Palace Gardens, lined by late nineteenth-century stucco or brick mansions, standing behind security fences and enveloped in private gardens. They are leased from the Crown Estate, and once housed embassies. Grade 1-listed Kensington Palace, which stands directly to the east of the site, has been a royal residence since the late seventeenth century and comprises work by some of England's most prominent architects, including Christopher Wren, Nicholas Hawksmoor and

above: Aerial view of Vicarage Gate House with its stepped terrace arrangement to the east, overlooking the residential fabric of Kensington Palace Gardens.

right: Vicarage Gate, north façade and entrance to the development.

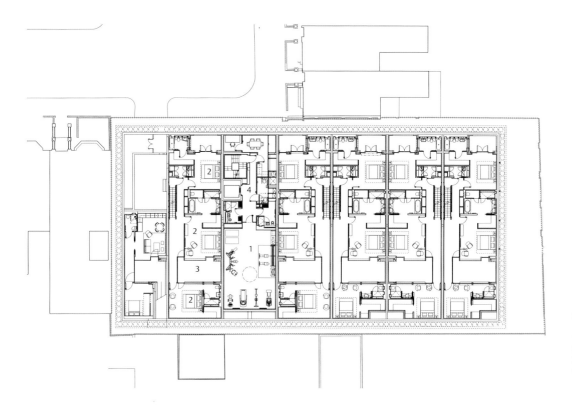

William Kent. Its wings and pavilions are made of two-shade red brickwork with stone and stucco dressings. The area to the south of the site is less rarefied, with a more village-like feel, as Vicarage Gate joins with Kensington Church Street and descends towards the busy shopping area of Kensington High Street. Saint Mary Abbots Church and Centre (the latter a lively, multipurpose venue) abut the southern boundary of the site. Further to the east and west lie the extensive open green spaces of Hyde Park and Holland Park respectively.

The site itself is at the junction of two nineteenth-century terraces, the leafy north-south Palace Gardens Terrace, and the east-west Vicarage Gate. The small green of Inverness Gardens faces the building's main façade. The site was once occupied by a Victorian church, which was severely damaged during the Blitz and replaced by an undistinguished nursing home in 1959. The latter's demolition in 2008 cleared space for the present development. The Victorian terraces to the immediate north and west are grade 2-listed, and an architectural language was sought which would give the new building a similar scale, character and richness of detail. Palace Gardens Terrace has stucco-rendered façades in an Italianate style, while the houses which abut the new building on Vicarage Gate are High Victorian. Both of these terraces are five storeys high, with consistent cornice lines and area wells enclosed by railings. Their rhythm of bay windows and entry porches identifies them as rows of individual townhouses, although most have now been converted into apartments. The formal ornate fronts hide plain brick backs with boxy vertical extensions, and a domain of courts and gardens. While the single-owner London townhouse is today mostly a memory, the residential terrace remains a highly successful and versatile type to be reinterpreted. The east boundary of the site is shared by Nos 9 and 10 Kensington Palace Gardens. Built around the turn of the twentieth century, these are detached red-brick mansions with Portland stone dressings and pitched roofs with dormers, standing in lush gardens.

The new building takes many cues from the adjacent façade of Vicarage Gate Terrace. Built of traditional London stock yellow brickwork with red-brick, stone, stucco and dark metal accents, this terrace has bay windows, entry porches, decorative brickwork details and mansard roofs with dormers above a deep cornice. The front façade displays a considerable thickness, with various elements either projecting from or recessed behind the primary face of the brickwork. The profiled white string courses and deep reveals around the windows create strong shadow patterns and a satisfying solidity, characteristic of traditional masonry.

left: View of the duplex lightwells at lower ground level with the balconies of the south façade above.

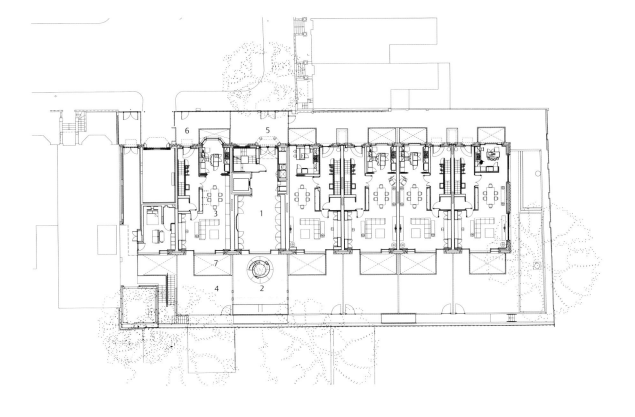

Ground Floor

1 reception
2 reception terrace
3 duplex living room
4 duplex garden
5 building entrance
6 duplex entrance
7 duplex lightwell

First Floor

1 stair core
2 lateral apartments
3 balconies
4 terrace
5 living rooms
6 bedrooms
7 master bedroom

N

0   10m

1:500

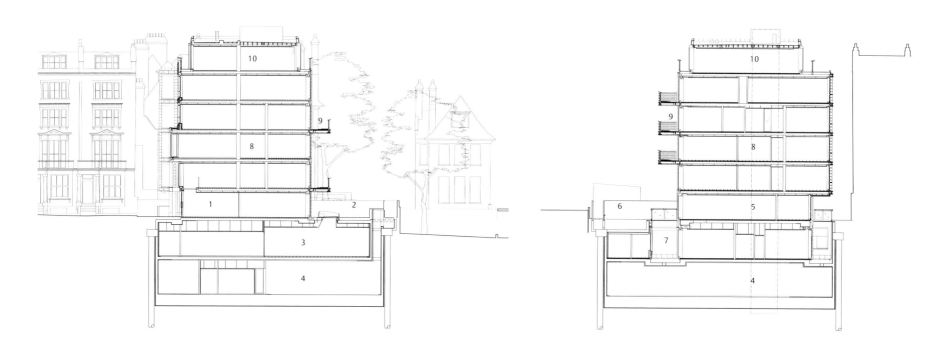

1 building reception
2 reception terrace
3 gym
4 basement carpark
5 duplex apartment
6 duplex gardens
7 duplex lightwells
8 apartments
9 balconies
10 penthouse

0 1   5   10m

1:400

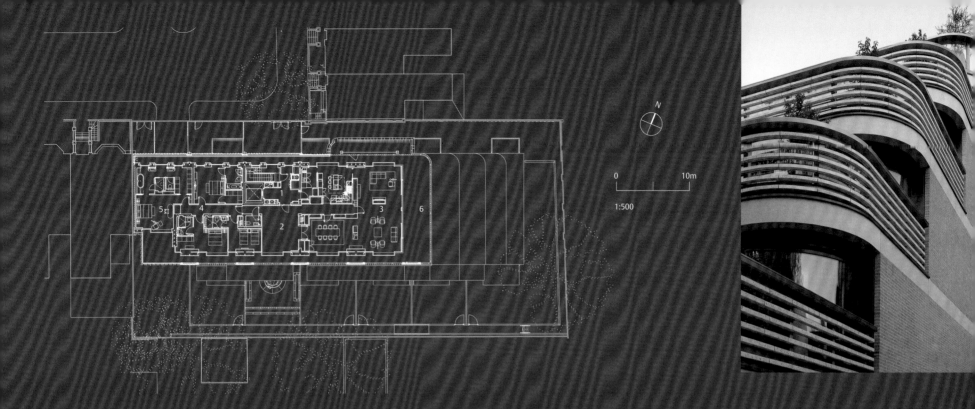

Vicarage Gate House restores the original line and order of the street. It is a concrete frame structure, clad in hand-made yellow brickwork, with cream-coloured polished or acid-etched precast concrete and ceramic accents, zinc mansard roof, and glazing in contrasting bronze-finish frames. It contains a mixture of duplex and lateral apartments. At the most visible western half of the front elevation, the structural bay rhythm is used to create the impression of a terrace of row houses. While the neighbouring terraces have five storeys, however, the new building has six. The careful manipulation of the section has allowed for the insertion in the lower half of another storey, which the continuation of the main horizontal lines has made barely noticeable. At ground level, the western-most bay contains the car lift and a path across the building. The third bay houses the stair and lift core, with a generous reception lobby and terrace. Below this shared terrace, and lit by a large oculus with a sculptural cast-metal railing, is the residents' gym. The other bays across the façade contain private street entrances to duplex units, marked by steel and curved-glass canopies. The duplexes have bedroom accommodation on the lower ground level, lit on both sides by generously proportioned lightwells. These units also have individual back gardens and have proven particularly popular with buyers. From the first floor up, there are only lateral apartments, accessed from the central core. The eastern side of the building steps back in a sequence of garden terraces, as the apartments become smaller. This stepped profile was an initial response to a concern about the visible bulk of the building from Kensington Palace Road but has become one of its defining features.

The dominant north façade of the building is a hybrid of at least two elevations: the west one, which is its chief face and which terminates the view along Palace Gardens Terrace, and the east portion, which is inserted behind and somewhat obscured by number 2 Palace Gardens Terrace. The former adjoins Vicarage Gate Terrace and consists of three formal, densely articulated bays designed to resemble a row of townhouses, with bay windows to the left and front doors to the right. The lower three levels have dominant upright elements – the white precast-framed bays and tall fenestration panels set into the wall – which create a strong vertical rhythm through a kind of giant order. Below these, the entrances are marked by shallow curved precast lintels. While an impression of individual houses is created, the first and second levels in fact contain large lateral apartments. The wall at levels 4 and 5 is flatter and more suggestive of continuous horizontal accommodation. The punched windows at these levels are set in recessed panels with precast lintels and cills. This 'body' of the building terminates with a precast parapet, which is part of the balustrade of the 'attic' penthouse level, where the envelope also varies according

to its position. The west three bays, visible from the street, have a traditional zinc mansard roof with three dormers between projecting zinc fins, suggestive of party walls. The dormers are embellished by delicate tapered precast frames. They change to full-height picture windows in the eastern bays. The impression of individual 'townhouse' bays is strengthened by two bronze-finish hoppers and rain downpipes which emerge from vertical recesses in the terrace balustrade. All these elements – the bays, entrances, windows and downpipes – recall the proportions and materiality of their nineteenth-century predecessors, interpreted in a modern idiom. The shortbread-coloured brickwork has a mellow softness which sits well beside the Victorian stock brick of the adjoining terrace.

The third formal bay contains the core and main entrance. Its communal significance is expressed by subtle alterations to the established pattern. The wider double entry door with ceramic handles is here placed on the left, within the bay window frame, which is now transformed into a kind of columnar portico. The opening below the curved lintel to the right becomes a window into the stair. The fourth bay is transitional and is set back one brick thickness behind the formal bays. It contains vertical bands of narrow and wider windows, the latter's main purpose being to give the eastern apartments a long view up Palace Gardens Terrace.

East of these, as the building slides into the lane and faces the somewhat rustic brick end wall, a distinctive projecting bay, clad in pale ceramic blocks, emerges. This unusual projection contains bedrooms and bathrooms and seems to be a way of celebrating the unique condition of this part of the building. Its west corner is formed by distinctive curved, full-height windows. This contrasts with the east corner, which is square. The projection is entirely clad in a rainscreen of mottled pale-grey ceramic cladding, introducing a new material which then continues clockwise around the building. It consists of alternating courses of rectangular blocks and more elongated, projecting ribs. This gives the projecting bay a sense of weight and tactility, somewhat reminiscent of rustication. In the classical tradition, rustication is generally expressive of the earthly origins of architectural order. Here, however, the suggestion of mass is leavened by the shimmer of the ceramic. The precast string courses are continued across this part of the elevation by slightly projecting ceramic bands. The available light is dispersed and reflected by the ceramic surface, giving it an interestingly dappled, changeable character. The curved, full-height windows on the west corner of this bay are a dramatic feature of the façade, maximising light and offering special views into the greenery of Inverness Gardens. The penthouse parapet in this more private part of the roofline turns from opaque to transparent, with a glass panel balustrade above the

ceramic bay. The two halves of the north façade are united by the row of duplex entrances, the continuous parapet and string courses, as well as the highly contemporary, two-colour steel railings which enclose the street-frontage lightwells.

The distinctive form of the east side of the building, with terraces which step back at each level, reduces its apparent mass but is also a contextual response to the world of back gardens. The terraces provide valuable amenity and privacy to the living rooms and master bedrooms of the apartments. The building envelope on the east side is almost entirely glazed, maximising the connection between the inside and outside. The terrace balustrades consist of a layer of clear glass, over which is superimposed a discontinuous veil of horizontal ceramic ribs. These pieces accentuate the horizontal direction and balance views with privacy. The curvature of elements on the north-east corner – the curved windows, balustrades and precast bands – recall Art Deco.

The south elevation is constituted by brick piers and vertical panels of floor-to-ceiling glazing, an arrangement meant in part to echo the row of vertical extensions on the backs of the adjacent Victorian terrace. The precast banding provides scale and continues the horizontal emphasis. The fenestration on this elevation, consisting of full-height picture windows flanked by sliding glass pocket doors, is a

distinctive feature. The regularity of this framework is counteracted by seven ceramic-faced balconies, which relate to the living areas of the apartments and form a playful pattern. The ground-level gardens on the south side of the building are punctured by a series of large lightwells, which create open-air courtyards in the lower-ground floor plan. They are a clever device which enables this accommodation to extend nearly to the site boundary, creating space above for south-facing gardens.

The apartments in the building are generally oriented with the main living and reception areas toward the south and east. The care which went into their design is apparent, for example in the large lateral units on levels 1 to 5 in the eastern half of the building. Here, the increased width created by the ceramic bay made it possible to have three parallel bands of rooms, with the more private domestic zone of bedrooms and bathrooms on the north side being comfortably separated from the more public southern domain used for entertaining guests. The north-east corner of these stepped units again receives a special treatment, with the full-height curved windows and corresponding curved terrace balustrades which make the most of the attractive garden views. There is thus a contrast here, as in the traditional terrace type, between a formal front and a more relaxed, private back.

As is typical for the practice, the sophistication of detailing and quality of execution are very high, and contribute significantly to the architecture's success. A manufacturer was selected who could produce handmade bricks by traditional methods to ensure a desired mellow texture and colour – after firing, the shortbread-coloured bricks take on a faintly pinkish glow. They also have elongated proportions resembling those of Roman bricks, in order to accentuate the horizontal direction (for this reason, the horizontal joints in the brickwork are also several millimetres wider than the vertical ones). To achieve a massiveness characteristic of traditional masonry construction, the brickwork on the front façade is at times three layers thick, with deep reveals on the wall surface. The bands of precast concrete are deep and – with the brickwork – self-supporting. Their finish on the front of the building is polished, bringing the reflective marble aggregate into sharper focus, while elsewhere it is acid-etched for a softer, velvety texture. The ceramic rainscreen cladding is semi-lustrous and oscillates in colour with the changing light conditions between bright, dappled white and shadowy grey.

The building's interiors are generous and well appointed. The joinery is of exquisitely crafted English oak. The simple stair railings, with a stainless steel structure and oak handrail and spindles, invite touch. The window assemblies, which occur mainly on the south elevation of the building,

are particularly sophisticated. Here a picture window positioned near the outer surface of the wall is flanked by two inset glazed pocket doors which slide with ease into the thickness of the wall behind glass railings. The internal oak frames have a level of finish associated with fine furniture. The effect is one of a handsome bay window with a strong connectivity between the interior and exterior space.

As with the other buildings in this volume, the design of Vicarage Gate House was shaped by a keen sensitivity to the numerous given conditions and urban traditions of the context. The resulting Ruskinian "changefulness" of the exterior treatments becomes part of the design approach, an alternative to abstraction or arbitrariness. There is a masterful architectural play between apparently conflicting modes – the load-bearing masonry tradition versus modern frame construction, the vertical 'townhouse' units versus broad lateral apartment – which results in their interesting reconciliation.

left: Detail of the curved corner bay windows on the north façade, which resolve the transition from the traditional London stock yellow brickwork to the white painted stucco of the neighbouring building with a bespoke ceramic cladding design.

right: Ceramic cladding of the curved corner on the west of the façade overlooking Vicarage Gate.

111 Buckingham Palace Road

In 2014 Eric Parry Architects was commissioned to remodel the entry area to an existing commercial office complex located on the west flank of the Grade II-listed Victoria Railway Station on Buckingham Palace Road... The architectural handling of the space and finishes evokes the elements of earth, horizon and sky which – with the suspended art installation – now suggest a great 'cosmic room'.

111 Buckingham Palace Road provides a startling demonstration of how a series of intelligent but relatively small interventions can completely transform a building's urban presence and the arrival experience for thousands of office workers. In 2014 Eric Parry Architects was commissioned to remodel the entry area to an existing commercial office complex located on the west flank of the Grade II-listed Victoria Railway Station on Buckingham Palace Road. The brief was firstly to create a new, more attractive entry behind an extant Edwardian stone screen. Secondly, there was urgent need to improve the existing congested and insalubrious conditions of the public pavements in front of the building on Buckingham Palace Road, which at that time was part of the Victoria infrastructure upgrade being carried out by Westminster City Council. The practice enlarged the dated and fragmented reception area by removing the narrow vehicular forecourt and extending the hall to the stone screen, which became its façade. The back-of-house facilities were cleverly remodelled at the rear of the hall, and a new reception area with a feature desk was located closer to the entrance at the south side of the hall. The top of the space was remodelled with a sloped zinc roof behind the façade parapet. A large new skylight was created above the reconfigured escalators zone on the east side, dramatically illuminating the new hall and a large mobile artwork commissioned for it. The spatial experience was transformed with the replacement

of the previous steep external steps with more generous, elegant ones which now create a transition inside the hall between the entry zone and the theatrically raised reception. The whole has been paved and clad in large-format book-matched slabs of lightly veined White Wenqe stone. The disabled ramp has been transformed from a mundane necessity to a monumental architectural element in its own right. The stone screen was cleaned and restored, and provided with high-quality revolving doors and glazing, the latter elegantly divided by mullions and transoms in a refined, human-scaled composition. The architectural handling of the space and finishes evokes the elements of earth, horizon and sky which – with the suspended art installation – now suggest a great 'cosmic room'.

The site is located on the eastern side of Buckingham Palace Road, directly south of the Victorian bulk of the Grade II-listed Grosvenor Hotel. This part of the block is circumscribed by the Edwardian Baroque stone and brick enclosure of Sir Charles Morgan's extension to the railway station, completed in 1908. It is now surmounted by a long shopping centre and office building built in the 1980s. Having a mirrored-glass façade, the complex extends to Eccleston Bridge to the south and to the raised service and taxi court to the east. The site's stone façade originally led to an external forecourt, which was used by vans accessing the station's parcel office and which had a frontage onto the station

above: Views of the pre-existing entrance forecourt.

opposite: Eric Parry Architects' proposal incorporated the pre-existing stone screen, making it the actual façade to the new-build

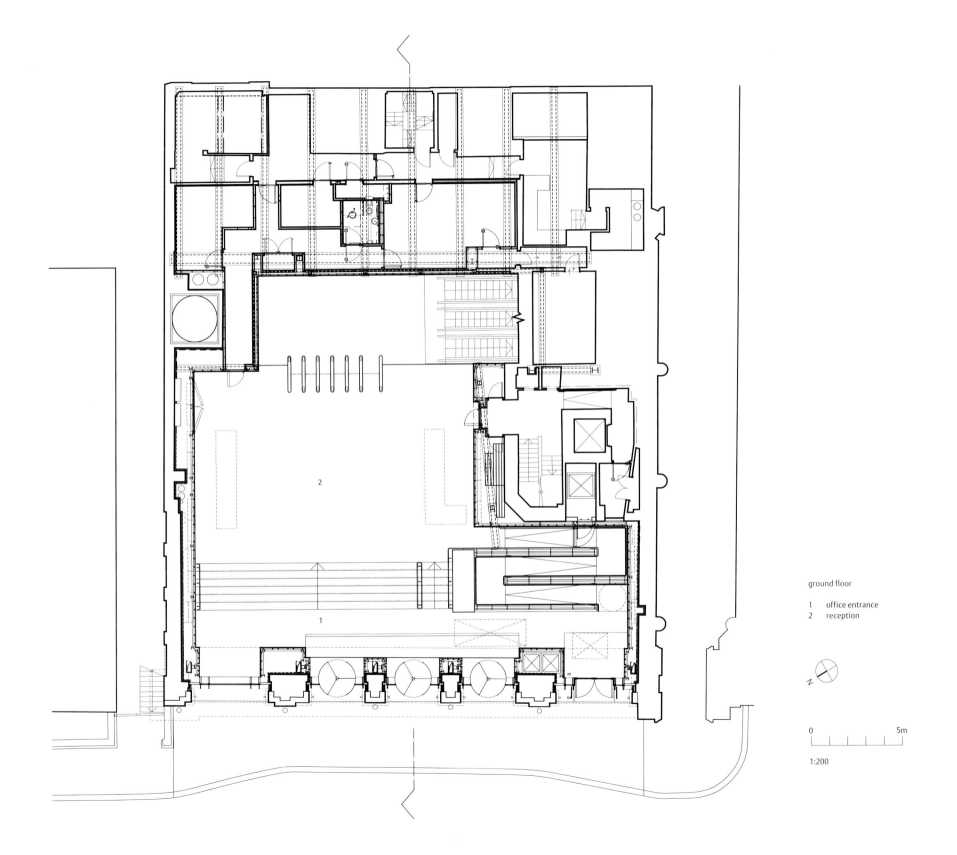

ground floor

1   office entrance
2   reception

0   5m

1:200

concourse behind it. The screen was quite radically modified in 1983, when the present five tall openings were created. The great Victorian railway stations, with their grand hotels, were exuberant celebrations of arrival and departure. The present building has similar aims.

The reception area built in the 1980s had a narrow vehicular forecourt with pavement crossovers, steep external steps and an obtruding vent column. The reception area itself was at the back of an oval hall of outdated decor, far from the entrance doors, with service rooms behind it. Eric Parry Architects created a simplified, large rectangular space, made possible by the elimination of the external forecourt and by extending the reception hall to the street wall. They also remodelled the back-of-house areas which now include new meeting and storage spaces as well as accessible toilets.

The handsome existing façade of 111 Buckingham Palace Road is made of Portland stone ashlar and is now Grade I-listed. It has been cleaned and carefully restored, and a new steel structure was inserted behind it inside the old court to construct the entry hall, giving the façade screen a substantial depth. It consists of three round-arched openings in the centre, flanked by two wider flat-arch openings, from which it is separated by rusticated pilasters. The subtly varied rustication of the piers and side arches, admirably adapted in the 1980s, articulates and

unites the whole façade. It gives it a sense of solidity which contrasts with the transparency of the large areas of new glazing and the natural light visible in the interior beyond. Capped by a dentil cornice and parapet, the façade recalls certain triumphal city gates (such as the Puerta de Alcalá in Madrid), an architectural type associated with ceremonial entry. The stylish new glazing in dark metal frames has been recessed within the deep arches, creating dramatic shadows. The various openings accommodate different uses. The three central arches contain new revolving doors, surmounted by uninterrupted glazing. These handle most of the pedestrian flow. The wider, right-hand opening holds a double, glazed door, framed by smaller glass panels, with the transom and mullions providing human scale. The dimension separating the mullions echoes the width of the three central openings. Leading to the foot of a ramp, the right door is intended primarily for disabled access. The left-hand opening has been internally formed as a deep bay window. It creates a quiet recess off the main hall and allows a clear view of the interior from the street. The street image is calm and elegant.

Inside the stone screen and highly visible from the street lies the generously proportioned, luminous new reception hall. Raised by five shallow steps above the level of the entry zone, it is slightly reminiscent of a podium or a stage, set for the drama of human interaction. A recessed shadow-gap 'horizon' divides the hall into a lower and an

left: Early morning view of the new-build, which has incorporated the pre-exsting screen, now the actual façade, marking the transition to the office entrance and reception.

right: View of the reception from the office entrance, leading to the escalators in the background.

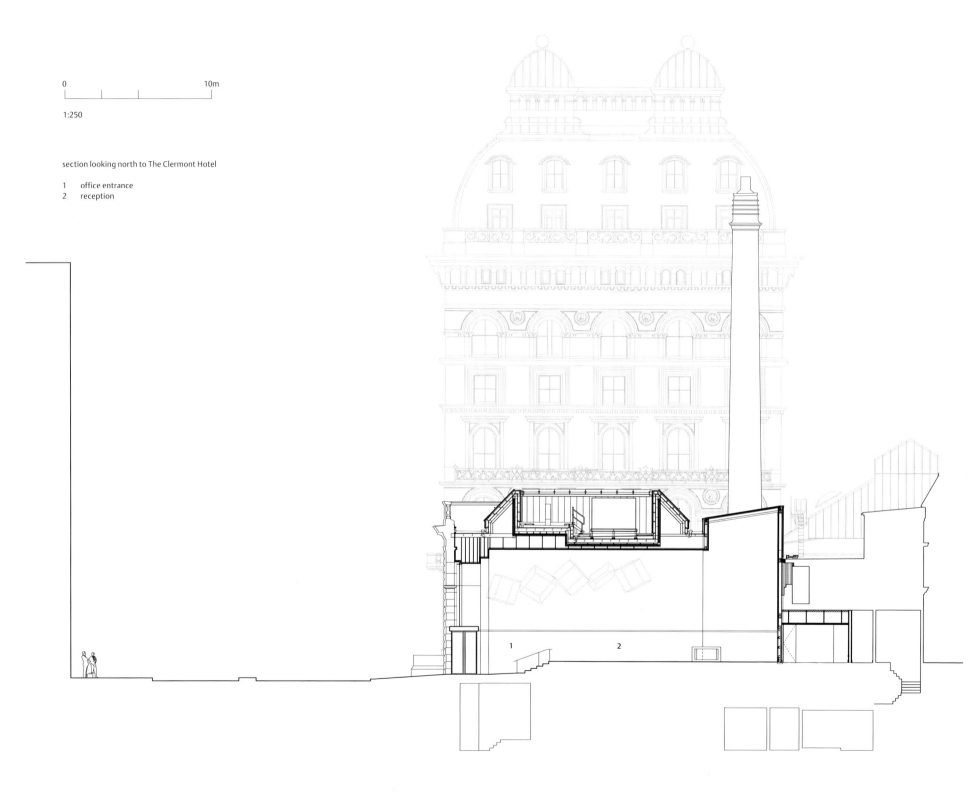

0   10m

1:250

section looking north to The Clermont Hotel

1   office entrance
2   reception

above left: Downward view of the transition from the reception to the escalators.

above right: Downward view from the top of the escalators descending to the space of the reception.

opposite: Northward section through Buckingham Palace Road with Clermont Hotel in the background and Victoria Station immediately adjacent to the east.

upper zone. The walls of the lower, 'earthly' zone are clad in large-format panels of Italian White Wenge stone. These rise to slightly above human height to align with the door heads. The doors on the north and east sides are suppressed, amplifying the impression of sheer stone walls. The horizontal boundary is continuous around all four sides of the hall, connecting the façade to the interior. The stone panels on the walls are vein-cut and book-matched, their subtle linear pattern emphasising the sedimentary nature of the material and creating continuous horizontal banding around the room. The upper portion of the hall is finished in reflective polished plaster, which lights up with the daylight flooding the space from the large skylight above the escalators zone.

The same stone is used as paving for the floor, stairs and ramps. The book-matched slabs on the horizontal surfaces are however cross-cut, exposing the surface of the natural strata. This means that instead of a linear pattern, the visible grain is curvilinear and meandering, suggestive of the spreading and gently rippling surface of water. Such metaphorical affinities between stone pavements and water are part of an ancient iconographic tradition, noted by Parry in his writings. This very exacting handling of the stone highlights the material's natural character and thematises the distinction between the room's vertical and horizontal planes. It is as if the lower portion of the hall had been carved out of the earth.

Other beautifully executed stonework details add to the room's thematic content. The panels behind the projecting reception area have vertical and horizontal perforations, which serve for heating, ventilation and sound attenuation. This pattern draws attention to this special area. The reception desk itself combines a cast-bronze enclosure with a thick, richly grained wood desktop, supported by delicate bronze legs. Below this horizontal wood plane, the reception desk enclosure is formed into large-scale grooves, reminiscent of the column fluting of archaic temples. The monolithic plinth which separates the steps from the ramp also recalls sacred sites. The architectural references in the reception desk are echoed by the vertical incisions in the stone behind it. The high quality of joinery and metalwork here are good examples of the practice's emphasis on craftsmanship and tectonic making.

One is inclined to see the entrance hall in terms of the architectural archetype of the 'cosmic room', with the highly tactile, patterned stone recalling the material's origins in the geological forces of earth and water, while the bright airy volume above is reminiscent of the celestial realm. This metaphorical reading is encouraged by the art installation above, commissioned by Modus Operandi Art for Kennedy Wilson, Eric Parry Architects' client, from the artist Claire Morgan. Created for this space, the vast aerial sculpture, entitled *Murmurations*, hovers below the ceiling, translucent and shimmering against the

light. Illuminated by star-like spotlights, it glitters in different colours, an uncanny evocation of the natural phenomenon which gives it its name. This ethereal artwork, set off by its luminous background and contrasting with the weightiness of the street façade, also forms an important part of the building's exterior image.

The stone wall cladding continues into the refurbished escalators zone in the south-east corner, where three escalators rise towards the existing office lobby above. In contrast to the entrance hall and upper lobby, the escalators area is enclosed, dark and cave-like. Its walls are clad in the vein-cut stone panels, their horizontal banding here accentuating the vertical movement of the escalator users. The upper portion of the walls and the soffit are finished in a polished dark plaster which animates the ceiling with reflections. The edges of the soffit are picked out in strip lighting. The journey thus proceeds from the bright and airy new reception hall below, through a moving, shadowy tunnel, to the old skylit lobby at the top.

The new 111 Buckingham Palace Road reception hall is another instance in which an architectural transformation has been accomplished within a sensitive historical setting. The resulting refined and highly theatrical architecture of the new intervention, like the Victorian railway station to which it is appended, celebrates the acts of arrival or departure. A few simple elements – top light, stone used in its elemental form, steps and a plinth – give this room a calm dignity.

above: Details of the bespoke reception desk.

opposite: Claire Morgan's permanent installation, entitled *Murmurations* (2016), which was commissioned for this space.

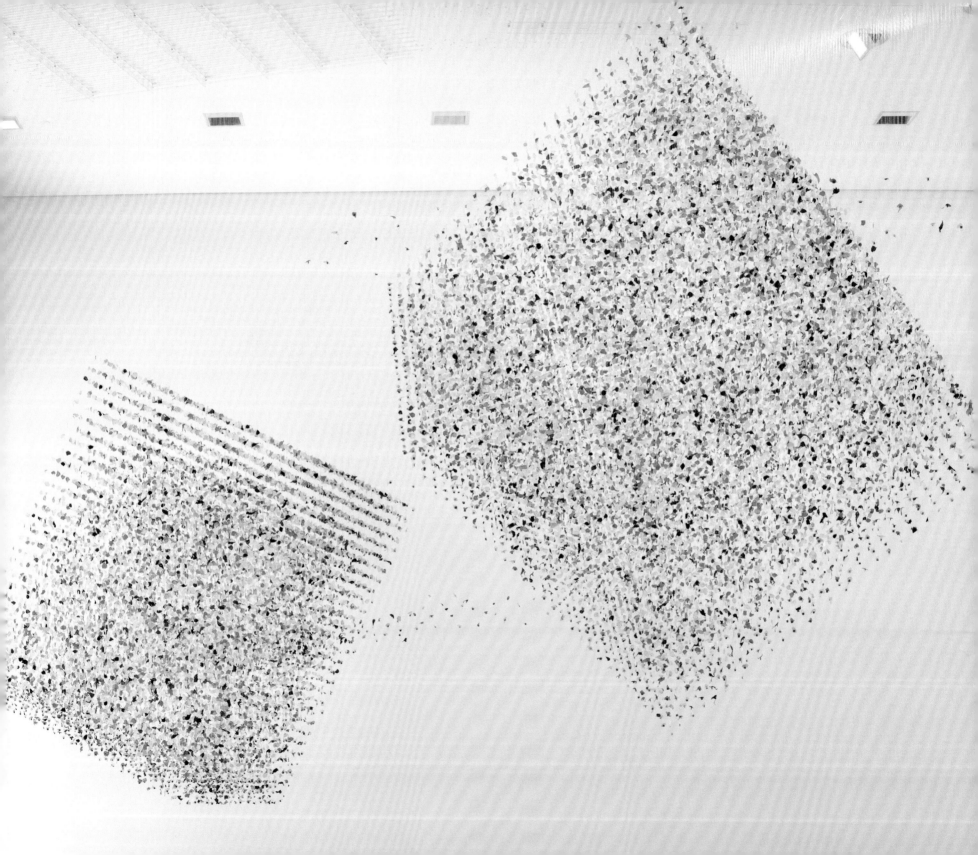

Sir John Soane's Museum Exhibition

'Eric Parry: Drawing' was the title of an exhibition at Sir John Soane's Museum, that was open to the public from 20 February to 27 May 2019. The exhibition was entirely designed by Eric Parry Architects, bringing together a selection of Eric Parry's hand drawings and notebooks. The exhibits selected covered more than four decades of architectural observation, design and construction.

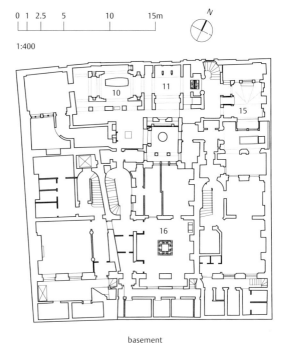

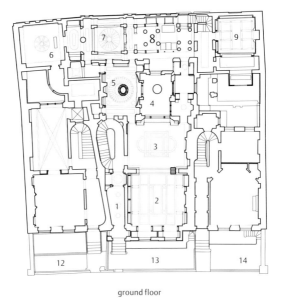

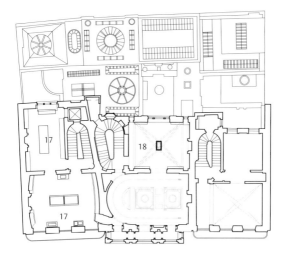

basement   ground floor   first floor

0 1 2.5   5   10   15m

1:400

N

In early 2019, an exhibition entitled 'Eric Parry: Drawing' was staged within the remarkable setting of Sir John Soane's Museum in Lincoln's Inn Fields. It brought together a selection of the architect's hand drawings and sketchbooks, spanning more than four decades of thought and practice. The exhibition was part of the Museum's programme of illuminating Soane's architecture by inviting notable artists and architects to create other layers around it. Drawing has always been a fundamental part of Parry's creative process, a feature shared with Soane. He has noted his aim of threading his interventions carefully into the existing context of the Museum, which accords with his own interest in how architecture exists in a broader continuum of the history of ideas. Parry's drawings in a variety of media were displayed in cases in the Museum's exhibition rooms, arranged around the themes of Observation, Design and Construction. In addition, five bespoke cabinets were designed by Parry for the display of his sketchbooks in other parts of the house, in ways that resonated with their specific settings. The exhibition also included a short film by Dirk Lindner and Alex Morgan, commissioned and produced by Eric Parry Architects, about their building at 4 Pancras Square. It followed its realisation from the drawing board through its extraordinary construction process and to its completion, evoking the dramatic and highly embodied nature of architectural making. A further intervention was made

in Soane's unique Picture Room with the strategic insertion of two photographic prints of the practice's buildings. The exhibition was accompanied by the publication by Sir John Soane's Museum of the book *Eric Parry: Drawing* (2019), containing texts by Parry, David Leatherbarrow and Owen Hopkins.

The Sir John Soane Museum is a unique institution, which has increasingly become a Mecca for architecture lovers in recent decades, since it was brought to the attention of new generations by Robert Venturi's seminal 1966 treatise *Complexity and Contradiction in Architecture*. While many of Soane's public buildings have now been lost, his house-museum – an architectural aggregate which he rebuilt and repeatedly modified between 1792 and his death in 1837 – is the most eloquent record of his architectural principles and experiments, as well as of his personal life. Different parts of the triple house served over the years as the Soane family home, while others were created for the education of students and the public about the art of architecture. The building and its collection were lovingly described by Soane in his 1830 guidebook, *Description of the Residence of John Soane, Architect*. It was part of his intention that the building remain exactly as he left it, so the arrangements of things have changed little since. Preserved here is Soane's professional office, where he practiced and taught architecture, and his idiosyncratic 'Museum',

1   Hall
2   Library
3   Dining Room
4   Monument Court
5   Breakfast Room
6   The Foyle Space
7   Dome Room
8   Colonnade
9   Picture Room
10   Catacombs
11   Crypt
12   No. 12
13   No. 13
14   No. 14
15   Monk's Parlour
16   Kitchen
17   Galleries
18   North Drawing Room

right: Small display on the Library table (Museum no. XF268), between the Dining Room and the Library, reflects on the task of listening with notes and sketches by Eric Parry made during lectures and conferences, and portraying fellow keynote speakers.

opposite: Plans of the entire Museum exhibition with the location of individual display cabinets.

comprising a remarkable collection of thousands of artworks, antiquities, models, drawings, books and architectural fragments. His own designs, often atmospherically presented in the paintings of his creative partner Joseph Gandy, became part of the story of the house. It is something of a microcosm of his larger projects, with subtle and complex layering of planes, rich colours and surprising, often thematic transparencies. Above all, it is a testament to his ingenious manipulation of natural light and shadow, the chief components of its unforgettable atmosphere. A complex network of apertures in the fabric – courts, lanterns and skylit slits – unexpectedly and with great theatricality highlights specific places and artefacts, and delivers yellow-tinted sunlight deep into the lower levels of the dense interior. The architecture often sets up unusual relationships between rooms, and the strategic use of round and rectangular mirrors sometimes creates the illusion of space extending far beyond the confines of the modestly scaled building. Both the structure of the house and of the collection were conceived thematically in oriented and variably meaningful space. This is evident, for example, in the way that the architectural drawing office (which hovers, unattached to walls, atop the colonnade at the back of the middle house) overlooks the deep, layered structure of the Dome-Museum area, a didactic resource for the draughtsmen who once worked there. Likewise, the subterranean realm of the basement level contains the gloomy,

medievalising Monks' Parlour, the Crypt and the Catacombs. Most importantly, Soane' house is deeply informed by a collagist sensibility. As a complex spatial assemblage, animated by theatrically modulated light and shadow, it derives its often unsettling poetic power from the use of creative juxtaposition. By placing contrasting fragments together and in conjunction with the architecture, Soane created a rich communicative space. It is thus not only a unique testament to the life and work of its architect, but an expression of his world.

Eric Parry's aim in designing the exhibition was to create a series of contemporary interventions, telling the story of his own creative process in a way which would resonate with the Museum's atmospheric setting. The placement of a number of new elements among the house's topography is in itself evocative of Soane's creative methods. There was also an autobiographical dimension. Parry's sketchbooks are an intimate document of his life, going back to his student days. They blend impressions of places and studies of architectural details with lecture notes and reflections, and include also sketches of friends and colleagues. They are as revealing of his life as Soane's house is of his. The sketchbooks were displayed in five new cabinets designed by Parry expressly for the exhibition, each having an interesting and sometimes surprising relationship with its context. They were situated in different rooms of the house, from the Kitchen and the Crypt in the

right: The Breakfast Room cabinet follows the outline of the oval breakfast table usually on display, presenting the visitor with a selection of notebooks and sketches reflecting on movement. The mirror at the centre of the cabinet reflects the elaborate ceiling.

basement, through the Breakfast Parlour and Library on the ground floor, to the North Drawing Room on the first. The cabinets bore a family resemblance and each was lacquered in a colour carefully chosen to match or complement Soane's own palette.

Parry's first cabinet was situated in the recently restored basement kitchen at the front of the house. This generous room has a rough flagstone floor and pale walls. The cabinet's form was inspired by the food preparation table, which normally stands in the middle of the room. It was here that Dalibor Vesely held his architecture seminars, while teaching at the Architectural Association in the 1970s. The sketchbook drawings in this case were oriented around the theme of character, both human (with evocations of distinctive faces) and architectural. The related notion of horizon was explored in landscape, buildings and whole city skylines.

The northern parts of the basement level were themed by Soane as the Underworld: dark and chthonic, with a palpable sense of depth and weight. To the west side are the Catacombs, where numerous Roman cinerary urns are encased in shadowy recesses. The area contains many other sepulchral objects, from the public (the ruined fragments of Soane's dismembered buildings) to the deeply personal (the memorial tablets to his deceased wife and eldest son). Parry's sketchbook vitrine

here was situated in the Crypt area at the back, below the colonnade and opposite the Monk's Parlour. It stood between two arches and was guarded by a pair of sombre casts of the Medici Venus. It also had an axial relationship with one of the most spectacular objects in Soane's collection, the luminous Egyptian alabaster sarcophagus of Seti I, visible in the Sepulchral Chamber at the heart of the Museum. Informed by the basement setting, with its muted daylight filtering through the ambient gloom, Parry chose for this cabinet drawings which explore the architectural play of light and shadow. The cabinet itself was a deep red, nearly square box with a clear cover. The open books were dramatically illuminated here by LED gantry luminaries, which made them appear to hover spectrally amid the shadows.

The Breakfast Parlour is one of the most distinctive rooms in the house, and highly characteristic of Soane's architectural style. A square at the centre of its plan is extended by the addition of rectangular layers of top-lit space to the north and south, a device which provides dramatic illumination for the works on the two walls and makes the room's boundary somewhat indeterminate. There are numerous surprising transparencies, through interior glazed panels into the Dome-Museum and stair, and through a window to the Monument Court. The room is crowned by a shallow dome. Springing from four segmental arches, it is supported by pilasters, so that the ceiling resembles a floating

canopy. The octagonal lantern at its centre brings in coloured sunlight. The ceiling and the arch soffits contain a number of small convex mirrors, which seem to fill the deceptively small room with fleeting reflections and transparencies, giving it a sense of animation and spatial ambiguity. The light and playful architecture of the Breakfast Parlour was important to Soane, who in his *Description*, presented it as "a succession of those fanciful effects which constitute the poetry of Architecture." Parry's cabinet for this room adopted the oval form and the central position of the breakfast table, reflecting the biaxiality of the room. A yellow-lacquered base displayed the sketchbooks under a clear oval cover. Its central cylindrical support, which appeared to pierce the table surface, was topped by a flat mirror, seemingly offset from its support by a strip of LED lights. This strangely'levitating'mirror pictured the moving visitors and multiplied the myriad reflections of the room. It also created the illusion of a deep void, which seemed to continue the vertical axis set up by the similarly proportioned lantern. The drawings displayed here were expressive of movement in dance, performance and also in architecture. The intervention resonated with the theatricality of the room. Two other new cabinets were similarly situated in the Library-Dining Room and in the North Drawing Room, and displayed sketchbook drawings themed around the notions of listening and learning in the former, and of urban history and precedent in the latter.

A different kind of intervention, exploiting the house's complex spatial relationships, was the mounting of two large Dirk Lindner photographs of 4 Pancras Square and Fen Court on the back of the outside panels of the south side of the Picture Room. This dramatically top-lit room in the north-east corner of the ground floor is famous for the ingenious way in which Soane's collection of drawings and paintings is mounted on the north and south walls on a series of hinged leaves. Opening to the inside of the room, these allow many works to be stored away from bright light, and to be displayed in a relatively small space. On the south side, when this movable partition is open, it lets indirect light enter laterally from the Monument Court. This also allows an oblique view – through another skylit slice of space, the Recess – into the area of the Monk's Parlour in the basement. One of the novelties of the painting storage in the Picture Room is its interactivity – the observer is bodily involved in moving the leaves into the light – which leads to a highly dynamic viewing experience. The photographs of Eric Parry Architects' work, mounted on the outer face of the south side of the Picture Room, both represented an inflection – one convex, one concave – of the buildings' façades. This, especially when seen from the perspective of the lower level, created an illusion of planes jutting forward and receding. That a spatial and optical play was intended is manifest in the fact that Parry's original idea had been to mount anamorphic

left: The double display cabinet in the Crypt may be viewed from either side.

above: View of the double-height space of the Monk's Parlour. The two photographs, printed on canvas, by Dirk Lindner, document Eric Parry Architects' buildings at 4 Pancras Square and Fen Court. The canvasses are held to the outside of the two panels opening into the Picture Room on the floor above.

right: In the North Drawing Room, complementing the height of the Dance Cabinet (Museum no. L110), a vertical two-tier display was designed to eye level (here seen from above).

drawings on the panels to be viewed from the Monk's Parlour. When opened into the Picture Room and seen head on, the effect of the fracturing of perspective's logic was even more powerful. In these ways, this simple intervention amplified the already rich and ambiguous spatiality of the architecture.

In the short video made to accompany the exhibition, Parry mused on the surprising and transformative nature of the imagination. While planning the exhibition, he had made repeated visits to the house, each time discovering new echoes and affinities. Parry's interventions in some ways parallel Soane's own imaginative process, where the latter's restless remodelling of his home and rearrangements of the collection constantly suggested new communicative relationships, which he would then be compelled to develop. What Parry described is the phenomenon of the thematic field which resides in the experiential world, where the imagination recognises latent connections between all kinds of – sometimes apparently unconnected – things.

This poetic sensibility, amplified in the intense atmosphere of the Soane Museum, also infuses other areas of the practice's work.

left: The north-facing gallery towards the rear of the building also included a display of individual chapters of the current *Volume* series, documenting each project. In the background, an easel with Eric Parry's original drawing for 4 Pancras Square.

above: In the south-facing gallery, or Front Gallery, completed by Caruso St John in 2012 and overlooking Lincoln's Inn Fields, a display of large and small hand drawings by Eric Parry, placing the emphasis on the detailing of architectural façades.

right: The Museum interior with a view of the Dome Room towards the Picture Room entrance in the background.

Lipton Residence II

Belonging to the Camden Conservation Area, the site area contains a number of the original 1840s white-stucco neoclassical villas. While the property's two immediate neighbours have been rebuilt as neo-Georgian facsimiles, Parry's aim was to create a contemporary reinterpretation of a Regency villa, which would relate to the style, scale and sensibility of the neoclassical precedents while also referencing the modernist heritage of north London.

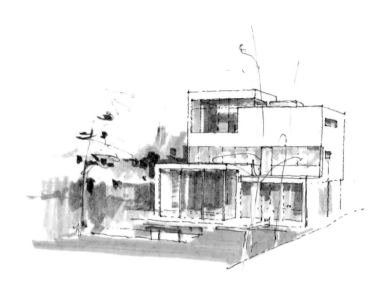

The second Lipton residence deserves attention in the practice's oeuvre as a rare example of a new house, and casts light on Parry's evolving thought about the theme of dwelling. In 2009 an approval was granted for a complete reconstruction of a 1930s neo-Georgian villa in north London's St John's Wood. The existing house on the site had been extensively remodelled by Eric Parry Architects for the same clients, Sir Stuart and Lady Lipton, almost three decades earlier. [See *Eric Parry Architects. Volume 1.*] The clients were very happy in the area, so when an opportunity presented itself to rebuild the house, they again approached the practice. In addition to creating a contemporary home in which to entertain and display the clients' growing art and ceramics collections, the brief this time included the provision of facilities for evolving family life (level access, adaptable bathrooms and a lift) and the requirement to reflect current standards of low-energy sustainable design. Belonging to the Camden Conservation Area, the site area contains a number of the original 1840s white-stucco neoclassical villas. While the property's two immediate neighbours have been rebuilt as neo-Georgian facsimiles, Parry's aim was to create a contemporary reinterpretation of a Regency villa, which would relate to the style, scale and sensibility of the neoclassical precedents while also referencing the modernist heritage of north London. The new building faces the street with a restrained, minimalist façade. By contrast, the back of the house is much freer and more expressive, with each of the principal rooms having a different volume and relationship with the two-level, lush back garden. The new landscaping, terraces and retained fishpond were completed in collaboration with Adriaan Geuze of the Dutch landscape firm West 8.

The elegant district of St John's Wood was first developed by the Eyre family estate in the first half of the nineteenth century. An early speculative development of detached and semi-detached cottages or villas on garden plots, it quickly became popular with artists, merchants and professionals looking for a retreat from busy city life, while having easy access to it. With its own chapel, assembly rooms and pleasure gardens, the St John's Wood development became the first suburban neighbourhood and was thus highly influential in the history of global urbanism. The extant Regency villas in the vicinity – now listed – are varied in form, but united by such characteristic features as their white stucco finish and vertical-format sash windows. Many have a rusticated ground level and a parapeted top which conceals the sloped roof. As the original houses aged, the area saw much rebuilding in the early twentieth century, generally in the neo-Georgian manner, using exposed brickwork. WWII damage led to a number of larger, modern blocks springing up, before the conservation area was established. In recent decades, many houses

above: Early sketches by Eric Parry for the street front and also the rear of the house, which overlooks the garden.

opposite: The rear of the house seen from the garden.

1:250

ground floor

1 hallway
2 sitting
3 garden room
4 kitchen
5 study
6 cloaks
7 tree pit and planting
8 terrace
9 courtyard below
10 garden bridge

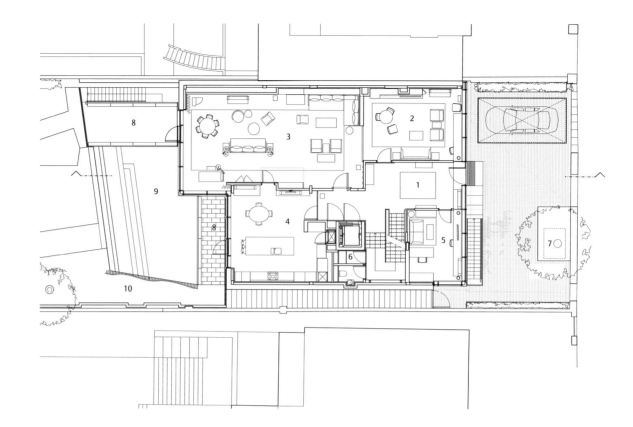

basement

1 lobby
2 dining
3 chair / table store
4 clothes store
5 china and silver store
6 larder / foodstore
7 vehicle lift
8 lift motor room
9 plantroom
10 full height acoustic louvres
11 planter pit above
12 refuse store above
13 entrance
14 laundry
15 store
16 serving kitchen
17 gym
18 court
19 planters
20 garden storage

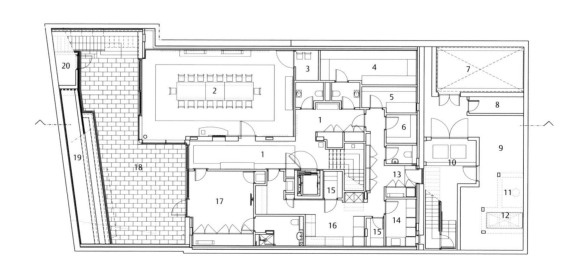

above: The hallway on the ground floor, here seen from the entrance, with the study to the left next to the stair; the corridor leading to the kitchen in the back and the garden room; and the sitting room through the door on the right.

right: Beneath the hallway, in the basement, the lobby leading to the dining room on the right and the garden in the back.

in the neighbourhood have undergone luxury remodelling in a range of historicist styles. The Regency villa type in its garden was seen by Parry as a significant contextual precedent, to be reinterpreted for clients with a sophisticated understanding of architectural discourse and a fondness for contemporary architecture.

The practice's earlier project on the site involved a comprehensive reorganisation of the spaces inside the existing brick envelope and the addition of a small, exquisitely detailed, travertine-clad extension at the back. This sat over a new lower ground level, containing a formal dining room with a close relationship to a sunken garden court. When complete reconstruction became possible, many of these successful features were redeployed. The first house had contained many finely crafted elements, such as cabinetry, solid Calacatta marble wash basins and beech doors with bespoke handles. A number of these pieces have been reused in fresh configurations in the new house. In addition to conserving resources as part of a low energy design, these fragments have become – together with the clients' artworks, designer furnishings and carpets – physical mementoes of a family history lived out in the earlier home. This somewhat collagist strategy reflects Parry's interest in the fruitful layering of the old and new as a means of creating a sense of memory and greater richness in a new construction.

The street elevation of the new house forms a backdrop to the sunny, hard-paved front garden, almost an urban *piazzetta*. Equipped with car and bins lifts, and paved in highly tactile granite setts, it is an uncluttered and somewhat theatrical space, which often causes passers-by to pause. The essentially neutral stucco panel of the upper façade appears to float above the independent glass and ceramic ground-floor layer, which provides animation and considerable transparency to the more public front rooms of the house. The generous entry hall is entered at street level, and flanked by the client's professional office to the left and a sitting room to the right. The partitions which divide the office from the hallway contain large glazed openings, so that it recalls a collegiate porter's lodge or a flight deck. With the resulting transparencies, it is as though the room was in the process of being pulled apart or assembled, thematising the act of construction. The office is closely related to the light-filled staircase, which at this point opens up the vertical dimension of the house. The detailing along the front wall of the ground floor is of a slender glazing screen stretched in front of structural *pilotis*. It recalls the villas of heroic modernism, a feeling which is accentuated in the entrance hall by grey and primary-coloured panels, layered with dark timber frames in a manner somewhat reminiscent of Purist or De Stijl interiors. The remainder of the ground floor contains the family kitchen and main living room,

each with a largely glazed back wall and its own terrace overlooking and connected to the upper garden. The keynote of the kitchen is sounded by the deep red of the monolithic granite countertops, and this is echoed on the exterior by a bold band of red on the kitchen's metal fascia. The interior design of the house was carried out in dialogue between Parry and the designer Chester Jones. This process is most evident in the stylish built-in furnishings. These are often combined with different types of timber panels, which also mask acoustic materials and heating grills. As with the reused door between the entry hall and living room, such panels are subtly asymmetrical, layered compositions, which thematise the passage from one room to another, provide sculptural accents, and anchor the doors with respect to the different ceiling height of each room.

The principal space of the ground level is the living area. A sliding partition divides the intimate sitting room at the front of the house from the grander living room at the back. The latter's ceiling steps up towards the garden, so that its volume projects above as well as beyond the kitchen. It has a sedum roof and a skylight which brings a dramatic shaft of natural light into the centre of the plan. The living room door is one of those reused from the earlier house. As with the others, it is placed in quotation marks, as it were, by its unusual assembly.

The suite of rooms on the lower ground level has an intimate connection with the deep garden court. It is a contemporary interpretation of a *sala terrena*, a zone which in Baroque palaces combined areas of entertaining guests with the iconography of grottoes and regenerative nature. The major room here is the formal dining room, which projects into the garden court with a glazed corner, its east side sheltered below the living room terrace. Its interior walls are again enriched with reeded timber panels, masking acoustic panels. The western side of the garden court is edged by the gym. The long corridor-anteroom which separates it from the dining room serves to bring daylight deep into the plan and – like the gallery of a country house – provides wall space for the display of paintings. These rooms open on to the garden court, which below the ground level becomes entirely clad in large-scale travertine. This porous sedimentary rock speaks of its origins in limestone caves and hot springs. Highly sensual, it is evocative of the mysterious metamorphic dialogue between earth and water. The upright cladding blocks are vein cut, while those of the paving are cut across the strata. This creates the impression that the whole of the garden court, with its massive stairs and terraced planters, has been carved out of the living rock. Top lit and partly hidden, the court shares many characteristics of an artificial grotto. In similar ways it suggests at the garden side of the villa the fusion of architecture and nature.

left: View of the stair on the ground-floor hallway, with the study in the back.

above: View of the study, which also overlooks the street.

right: In the basement, the dining room overlooking the garden, with the lobby to the left.

150

left: The sitting room on the ground floor, which greets the viewer to the right of the hallway.

right: The kitchen on the ground floor, overlooking the garden.

The upper two levels of the house comprise mostly bedrooms. The first floor contains an extremely well-appointed master suite, fitted out with finely detailed cabinetry and cream lacquer panelling. Running parallel to the bedroom, the generously proportioned master bathroom stretches the full depth of the plan. The grey-veined, white Calacatta marble covers the entire west wall and lends drama to the shower. The solid marble basins here and throughout are fragments imported from the previous house. With metal legs and towel bars, they are designed to stand somewhat independently, in a way which recalls freestanding Regency washstands, updated for the twenty-first century. Other such mementoes include the his-and-hers Eileen Grey mirrors which also multiply the reflections of the marble veining. The three very different rooms at the front of the first floor run behind the identical windows of the upper stucco façade. Circulation from one to another is parallel to the façade and creates a kind of *enfilade*, reminiscent of neoclassical precedents.

The contrast between the treatment of the street front and the back garden side of the villa is an important part of the design strategy. Following historical precedents, the minimalist street façade is a picture of elegant restraint, containing, however, some subtle architectural games. It consists of a two-storey, five-bay stucco panel set above a largely glazed ground-floor band. The former is flat and symmetrical, with two rows of identical, portrait-format tilting windows set nearly flush with the white stucco, expansion-joint-free wall surface. With the window proportions here suggesting a load-bearing wall construction, this stucco panel appears heavy. It seems to hover over the largely glazed base of the ground floor, which is recessed below it. As if to emphasise a structural independence, this lower band has its own eight-bay rhythm. The solid band above eye level and the waist-high spandrel are clad in cream-coloured ceramic panels, hand-cast for a rich tactility. They bring to the façade a durable, reflective and mellow finish, in addition to referencing modernism's thematisation of sunlight and the clients' love of pottery. The scale of the glazing and ceramic units is such as to suggest classical rustication, dematerialised here into a ghostly memory. The central two bays of the glazed screen correspond to the entrance hall and are marked by a simple aluminium canopy, which casts a deep shadow over the two-bay entry. The asymmetry of the front door, a subversion of the classical precedent, hints at the modernist spatial arrangements of the interior. Supported on *pilotis*, with a glazing module unrelated to the window rhythms above, and having horizontal emphasis, the glazed ground floor proclaims itself to be a Corbusian 'free façade'. The dialogue between the upper and lower zones lends this façade much of its architectural interest.

above: View of one of the
bedrooms on the second floor and
the bathroom on the first floor
adjacent to the master bedroom.

The restrained boxiness of the front is strongly subverted by the rear
aspect of the house, where the volumes of the major rooms are allowed
to jut up and out, forming individual relationships with the terraces and
gardens. Such differentiation between a formal front and more relaxed,
private back has long been part of the decorum of urban architecture.
This design strategy may also be seen, however, as an expression of the
modernist ethos of 'breaking out of the classical box', and the advent of
flowing and ambiguous modern spatiality. The private garden plays an
essential role in the configuration of the back. It is at two levels, that of
the terraces, bridges and original garden with fishpond, and that of the
sunken court. An inventive use of the latter as a way of bringing natural
light into the lower reaches of a building has developed into something
of a tradition in the work of the practice.

Rooted in part in the Modern Movement, the new Lipton residence is
somewhat reminiscent of Le Corbusier's 1924 Maison Plainex in Paris.
That purist villa faces an urban boulevard with a restrained, near-
symmetrical screen façade resting on *pilotis* over a glazed commercial
ground floor. By contrast, the rear elevation is more relaxed and open,
connecting the house by a bridge, and open staircase to a walled rear
garden at the *piano nobile* level. The Plainex was one of the architect's
early artist's studio houses, which he saw as research prototypes for the
modern urban dwelling. It seems fitting that Parry's current project for
a client who plays a key role in the construction industry, should explore
similar architectural themes.

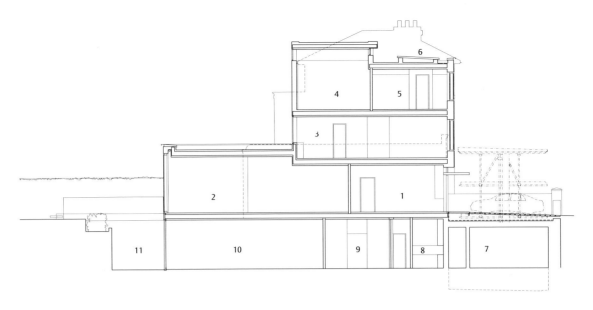

section

1   hallway
2   living
3   master bedroom
4   playroom
5   bedroom
6   solar water heaters
7   plantroom
8   laundry
9   lobby
10   dining
11   lower courtyard

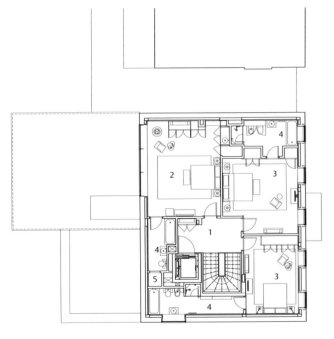

2nd floor plan

1   stair hall
2   studio room
3   bedroom
4   bathroom
5   whole house vent unit

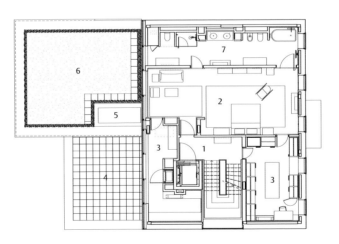

1st floor plan

1   stair lobby
2   master bedroom
3   dressing room
4   flat roof
5   rooflight
6   sedum roof
7   bathroom

0   1   2.5   5m

1:250

On the ground floor, the
garden room, overlooking the
garden towards the northwest
of the house.

Cambridge University Press & Assessment

Combining elegant, elongated wings with landscaped gardens, the Triangle, as the building is also known, now announces the arrival to the university city with a luminous beacon tower, crowned by a thematic artwork. As with other of the practice's projects, this large office complex is made distinctive by its formal inventiveness, the high quality of its making and by its attunement to its context, both physical and cultural.

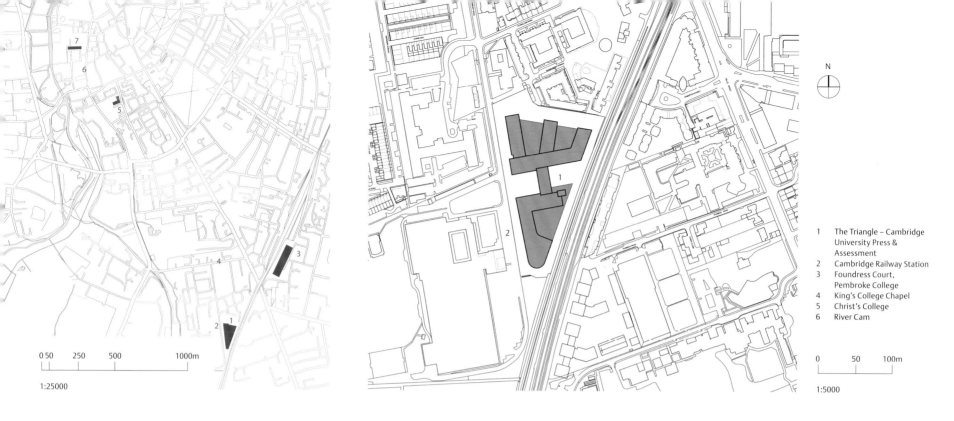

1 The Triangle – Cambridge
University Press &
Assessment
2 Cambridge Railway Station
3 Foundress Court,
Pembroke College
4 King's College Chapel
5 Christ's College
6 River Cam

1:25000

1:5000

For many decades, one of the abiding, slightly incongruous impressions of arriving in Cambridge by train had been the looming presence of the Cambridge University Press warehouse by the side of the railway line. For future generations of residents, students and visitors, this underwhelming experience has now been transformed with the construction of Eric Parry Architects' new 38,000m² headquarters for Cambridge University Press & Assessment. Combining elegant, elongated wings with landscaped gardens, the Triangle, as the building is also known, now announces the arrival to the university city with a luminous beacon tower, crowned by a thematic artwork. As with other of the practice's projects, this large office complex is made distinctive by its formal inventiveness, the high quality of its making and by its attunement to its context, both physical and cultural. Resonating with the collegiate architecture nearby, it comprises a series of shallow-plan 'fingers', containing meeting rooms and workspaces. These are structured around several calm, landscaped outdoor courts, providing visitors and staff with a restorative contact with nature. Its materiality of mellow beige brickwork and acid-etched precast concrete echoes the warm, tactile brick and stone architecture of the colleges and also that of some of the most successful of the city's contemporary developments. The building's different elevation types reflect representational and functional requirements as well as a responsiveness to its orientation

and immediate surroundings. It can also be seen as yet another of Eric Parry Architects' inventive investigations into the nature of the contemporary workplace as an architecture of civic, sustainable and biophilic character.

Cambridge Assessment, which manages the university's three exam boards, is one of the city's largest employers. Staff from numerous offices around the city have been brought together in the new headquarters which, with future growth, is expected to become home to between 2,500 and 3,000 staff. The organisation is an important and lucrative branch of the university's business, with an extensive global reach. The confidential nature of the setting and marking of examination papers required a secure building. The character of the work also called for ample space for collaboration and good potential for expansion within the new structure. The building is located in the Cambridge University Press campus, across the tracks from the main railway station in the southern portion of the city. The area immediately adjacent to the station has in the last decade been undergoing a major redevelopment which has aspired to creating a new gateway for the city. While the CB1 masterplan stipulated a distinctive quarter and significant regeneration with a lively mixture of commercial and residential accommodation, the results on the ground have so far been disappointing. The generic deep-plan office

Hand-drawn orthogonal
projection by Eric Parry, looking
over the entrance courtyard by
Shaftesbury Road.

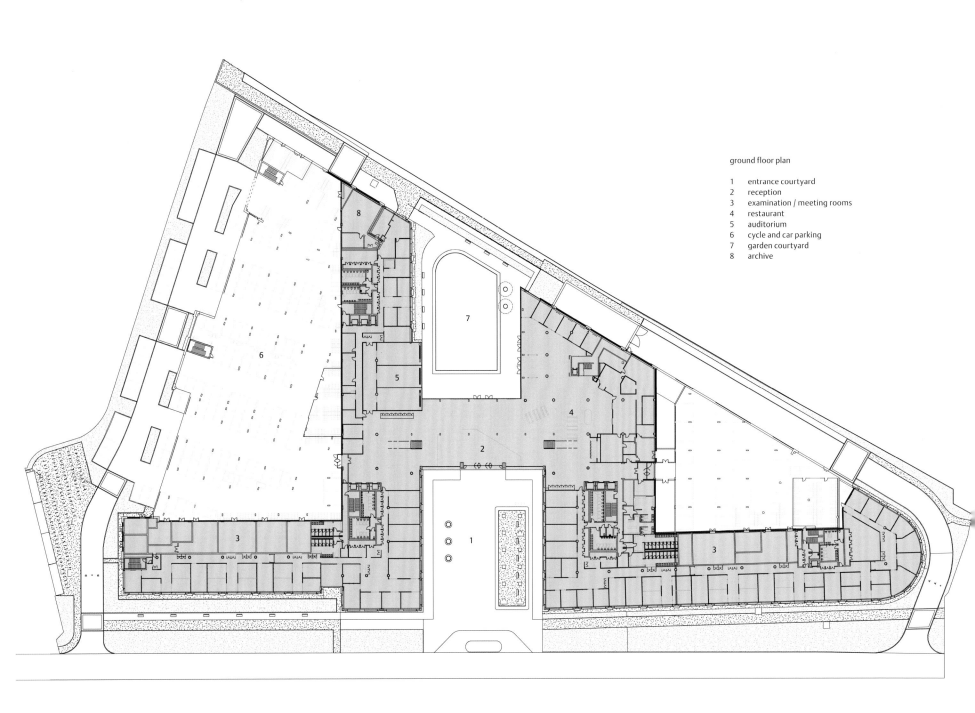

ground floor plan

1   entrance courtyard
2   reception
3   examination / meeting rooms
4   restaurant
5   auditorium
6   cycle and car parking
7   garden courtyard
8   archive

1:1000

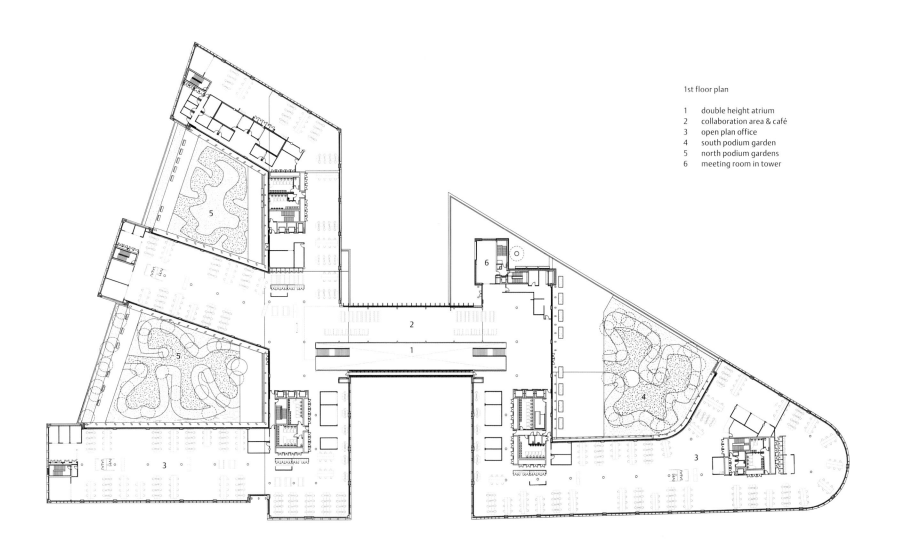

1st floor plan

1   double height atrium
2   collaboration area & café
3   open plan office
4   south podium garden
5   north podium gardens
6   meeting room in tower

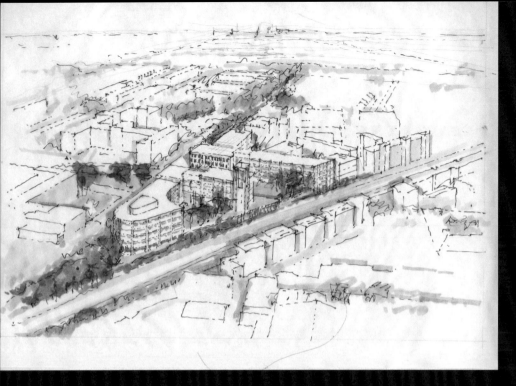

buildings which border a largely car-oriented new Station Square, and undistinguished rows of student housing with little green space, have failed to provide the needed design quality and civic atmosphere of a gateway appropriate to a renowned centre of learning. The new building counteracts some of these shortcomings.

The site of Cambridge Assessment is a north-south oriented triangle of land bordered by the railway line to the east, large-scale offices and the printworks of the Cambridge University Press to the south and west, and fine new housing, including the Stirling Prize-winning Accordia development, to the north. The building occupies the entire site and is visible from all sides. Its front elevation faces Shaftesbury Road, formerly a mainly residential street with many large brick houses, now mostly converted to institutional use. The railway side of the triangular site is perhaps its most prominent aspect.

The planning of the large perimeter building recalls the collegiate models of linear blocks enclosing semi-private outdoor spaces, but with an efficient, central entry. The Triangle has been conceived as a series of four and five-storey interconnected buildings, divided into two main blocks by a generous open space. The southern block

with respect to its context, so as not to compete with the city's existing towers. With its thematic artwork, it acts as a luminous beacon, becoming a familiar landmark which announces arrival to the millions of visitors who come to the city by train. The wider, northern block comprises three office wings. The two blocks are linked by a lower, bridge-like structure, which divides the central open space into an entrance plaza facing the street and a private garden beyond. It addresses the plaza with a representational screen façade of glazed-brick piers, which holds the blue fritted-glass panels of the integral artwork. The complex building contains four main service cores.

Arriving at the building from the north on Shaftesbury Road, one walks along its long front, embellished by landscaping and a rich variety of newly planted trees. The northern, lower portion of the front block is slightly set back, allowing for a linear planter along the pavement. Planted with grasses, this helps to screen the ground-level meeting rooms. The north block rises to five storeys and steps forward, announcing the symmetrical entrance plaza. From this point, the front of the south block has been slightly inflected. The shift is barely perceptible, but it neutralises what might otherwise have been a dauntingly long perspective view. With the tower

civic place. The glazed-brick entrance screen leads into the double-height reception hall. The conspicuous elements here are a pair of sculptural, fair-face concrete staircases with open precast treads, and stainless steel and glass balustrades. Their symmetrical arrangement lends a certain grandeur to the hall. The outer edges of the ground floor contain 77 meeting rooms of different sizes, many divisible by sliding partitions. Here visitors come to take part in the confidential examination processes. The centre of the plan provides staff and visitor catering, with access to the garden court. These spaces, and that of the café on the first floor, encourage the needed informal collaborative interaction. The ground level also contains an archive and an auditorium with a connection to the garden court. The areas beneath the podium gardens, lit by skylights, are used for bicycle and car parking. A landscaped strip along the east elevation contains a guided busway, provides access to bicycle parking and the garden court, and acts as a buffer against the railway.

The first floor contains a further collaboration area and a café overlooking the reception hall. From here, staff get a close view of the blue, fritted-glass artwork on the entry screen. The shallow office wings each have views and direct access to the podium gardens. The building's ecologically friendly, sustainable design is very evident here, with operable panels in the glazing for natural ventilation, and service beams which provide cooling when needed. The tower also emerges at this level on the railway side of the garden court. It contains six levels of distinctive meeting rooms below a viewing terrace.

The artwork, specific to the institution and its location, was again commissioned from the artist duo of Vong Phaophanit and Claire Oboussier. Called *In Other Words*, it thematises knowledge as understood in some of Cambridge Assessment's 160 client countries. The layered writings are digitally printed on the inner side of the double-glazed units. The work consists of two parts. It welcomes the visitor as the cool, blue-printed glass panels integrated into the glazed-brick entrance screen of the building's entrance courtyard façade. It also hovers above as the golden lantern of the tower, where the warm saffron and yellow colours of the texts collectively evoke the hues of ancient papyri and parchments. According to the artists, "the printed images are made up of multiple strata of coloured text, layers of colour gradations and script formations that form a complex 'palimpsest' …. Up close, fragments … of different languages are partially discernible. From a distance, the image reads more like a painting, the lines of text presenting as a shimmering mass of colour". In some areas of the glass, the printed textures dim almost to nothing, conjuring up the fading and fragmentary nature of ancient documents and of cultural memory itself. The content of

the text is based on the multilingual responses to the question "What does knowledge mean to you?" The resulting piece has the collected answers symbolically entwined into a unified image.

As with much of Eric Parry Architects' architecture, the building takes its cues from its orientation and physical context, and these are also reflected in its elevations. There are at least seven major façade types here, each responding to a set of conditions and giving a distinct expression to a particular part of the building. The complex whole is unified by the continuous material palette of mellow beige Leicester brickwork, hand-set in lime mortar in horizontal bands. These bands alternate with the fenestration, framed by cream-coloured, acid-etched precast concrete column casings and lintels. The façades are all deep and recessive, ranging in thickness between 400 and 900mm. They are animated by the play of light and shadow.

The main street façade is characterised by the large, slightly projecting windows of the meeting rooms, set between brick piers which – with each seventh course slightly recessed – recall classical rustication. This gives the outer façades an appropriate sense of rugged solidity. The solid panels, which conceal the sliding room dividers within, are expressed as vertical mirrored strips bisecting the ground-level windows and give the meeting rooms added privacy. The office-level

glazing has its own rhythm, created by slender, solid operable panels. The rhythms of the powder-coated metal window frames are enriched by the superimposed order of anodised aluminium brise-soleil. These solar shading screens vary from one part of the building to another according to differing levels of sunlight. They also enrich the abstract patterns of the fenestration.

The link building faces the entrance plaza with a glazed-brick entrance screen, the most elaborate and representational of the façades. Here the brick rustication of the front piers is echoed, with the recessed course now being of black glazed brick. The piers support a deep, stepped glazed-brick transom. Above it stands a row of 14 mullions, made entirely of highly tactile, handmade glazed bricks and capped by free-standing, decorative finials. The colours of these hand-set brick fins are subtly graduated from dark indigo at the bottom to creamy white at the top. The finials, which during the design process became more overtly face-like, give the fins a more explicitly anthropomorphic form. The screen thus resembles a row of caryatids, sentinels guarding the building's entry and the examination process itself. The different shades of blue in this screen allude to the blue ink of academic tradition. The theme of language and writing is further evoked by the layers of text within the glazing.

above and opposite: Two aspects of the south podium garden: the hard and soft landscape were the result of a collaboration between Eric Parry Architects and landscape architects Grant Associates.

The façades of the office fingers which enclose the podium gardens are very different again. Here the largely glazed office wall is overlaid by precast loggias separated from it by narrow stainless-steel-mesh maintenance walkways. The façades thus become very deep. The loggias serve to provide solar shading to the interior, while giving the garden elevations a rich and changeable texture. Because of the complex shape of the building, the colonnades of the loggias are highly variable depending on their location, with both the interval and plan profile of the posts informed by the M&E consultant Max Fordham's computer modelling of the building's daylighting and solar gains.

The elevations of the tower help to mark it as a beacon of arrival, with a less pronounced expression of the lower floors and an emphasis on its verticality. The two levels just below the viewing platform are articulated to give the impression of one tall volume, with a suppressed floor line and dramatic vertical accents. The viewing terrace reads as a shadowy gap, above which the translucent lantern appears to levitate.

Parry's tower as a civic landmark deserves further reflection. Representational towers are rare in the modernist tradition, where monumentality and symbolic content were often viewed with suspicion. The extreme height of today's urban skyscrapers is generally more expressive of status and land values than of civic intent. As the Cambridge Assessment building's security requirements and suburban location necessarily make it somewhat insular, its participation in the wider civic realm is chiefly through its tower. The majority of Cambridge's towers either belong to churches and college chapels or have taken the defensive form of college gatehouses. Perhaps the most comparable is the 17-storey tower of the University Library, built by Giles Gilbert Scott in the 1930s. Added to the design at a late stage to lend the large building the requisite recognition factor, it houses the book stacks and is visible from long distances. By contrast to Parry's, the University Library has a symmetrical and somewhat authoritarian Beaux-Arts plan, with the tower marking its central axis. Since the building of church towers was replaced by the construction of observatories, power stations and office high-rises in the modern era, most towers have arguably been the by-products of instrumental concerns. This was the case with Scott's iconic power stations, where the towers were chimneys, their scale needed to exhaust smoke high above the city. While the Cambridge Assessment tower also fulfils a utilitarian function (housing meeting rooms, viewing terrace, kitchen exhaust and plant room), its abstract composition and civic role suggest a kinship with such early twentieth-century Expressionist icons as Mendelsohn's Einstein tower, or Gropius and Meyer's Chicago Tribune project, the latter also asymmetric and vaguely anthropomorphic in form.

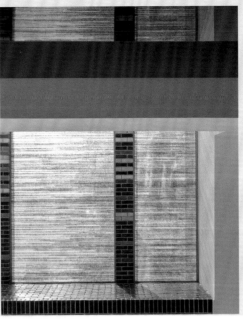

The artwork of Vong Phaophanit and Claire Oboussier punctuates the tower with light and the first floor of the south courtyard and reception with a work entitled *In Other Words*, which incorporates multiple layers of text into the glazing.

With his interest in cultural continuity, Parry has suggested an affinity between the Cambridge Assessment building and some of the highly crafted and civically generous mid-twentieth-century northern European institutional buildings, and in particular Alvar Aalto's National Pensions Institute. In that project, the architect addressed the challenge of a large urban office building in a similar way, by dividing the brief into a series of interconnected, elongated blocks, arranged on a triangular urban site around several open courts and landscaped terraces. The complex uses a similar material palette and is also punctuated by a tower element. The materials and workmanship are of a high quality, rare in British architecture in the immediate aftermath of the war. Aalto's oeuvre belongs to an alternative, highly contextual and craft-oriented tradition within the Modern Movement, popularised within Cambridge architectural circles by the work of Colin St John Wilson. Parry's sensibilities, manifest in the Cambridge Assessment building, share many common themes.

Parry's view of brickwork as a dignified material suitable for major buildings is also rooted in his understanding of the highly crafted Hanseatic brick tradition. The *Backsteingotik* developed over many centuries in northern and central areas of Europe and was deployed in both sacred and secular public buildings, such as town halls. These buildings, usually stripped of any figurative sculpture, derive their

authority and richness chiefly from the colour, texture and patterns of hand-set plain or glazed brickwork, sometimes supplemented by ashlar accents. This, together with the rich local collegiate tradition of brickwork, informed the material palette of Cambridge Assessment.

The Cambridge Assessment building is another of the practice's explorations of the potentials of the contemporary workplace, this time in a medium-height perimeter block, which provides a pleasant, characterful work environment with excellent daylight and connection to landscaped outdoor space. The deep, varied and highly articulated brick and precast façades reflect the functions and orientation of the interior, while relating to adjacent conditions. With its exploitation of passive solar cooling and natural ventilation, it is highly energy-efficient and sustainable. But its sustainability lies also in the quality of its making. The general expectation, in this ancient university context, of building things so that they endure is arguably the best strategy for responsible new development.

left: View of the building complex from Shaftesbury Road, looking south.

right: Aspect of the façade overlooking the south podium garden.

Chelsea Barracks

As might be expected for such a prestigious project, where an aura of expensiveness was one of the requisite qualities, the Phase 4 buildings manifest a very high quality of materials and handcraft. This is obviously true of the ashlar stonework. All meticulously formed and laid with consistent, narrow lime mortar joints, it was designed with deep reveals to evoke the solidity of traditional stone construction.

0 10 25   50   100m

1:4000

N

Phase 4
0   Five Fields Square
1   Eric Parry Architects, 1 Five Fields Square (Building 8)
2   Eric Parry Architects, Ranelagh House (Building 7)
3   Eric Parry Architects, 9 Mulberry Square (Building 6)

Phase 1
4   Mulberry Square
5   1 Mulberry Square
6   8 Whistler Square
7   9 Whistler Square
8   Whistler Square

Phase 2
9   Whistler Square Townhouses
10   Mulberry Square Townhouses

Phase 3a
11   8 Mulberry Square
12   The Restaurant At Chelsea Barracks

Phase 3b
13   retail
14   Garrison Square
15   The Garrison Chapel

Phase 5
16   Phase 5a
17   Phase 5b

Phase 6
18   Eric Parry Architects, Building 18 (Phase 6a)
19   Eric Parry Architects, Building 19 (Phase 6a)
20   Eric Parry Architects, Building 20 (Phase 6a)
21   Phase 6b

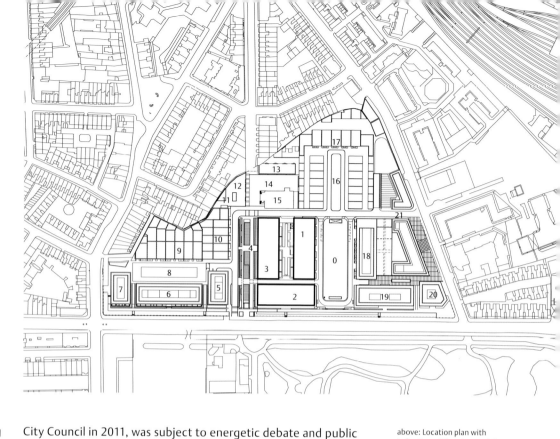

above: Location plan with indication of the phases of site development.

The Chelsea Barracks development is arguably one of the most interesting and ambitious housing schemes currently under construction. While aimed at the super-prime investment market, its emerging strengths and shortcomings will provide useful lessons to the wider debate about the making of cities. In the spring of 2015, Eric Parry Architects won a limited competition to design the Phase 4 grouping of residential buildings within the new Chelsea Barracks Masterplan. Its three apartment blocks form the edges of two publicly accessible garden squares – Mulberry Square and Five Fields Square – and enclose a private garden court. They comprise 98 luxury apartments and a residents' sports centre, spa and parking. Phase 4 also includes the design of Five Fields Square, the largest landscaped open space on the estate.

The redevelopment of the former Chelsea Barracks site has been famously controversial. With the decommissioning of the military installation, an unusually large piece of land in the most desirable part of west London became available. It lent itself to an ambitious vision, on the scale of some of the most successful and memorable residential developments produced by the great London estates during the Georgian and Regency periods. At the beginning of the twenty-first century, it is fitting that an urban development should be attempted which would be paradigmatic of best contemporary practice. Following the political interventions surrounding the rejection of the RSH+P scheme, the new masterplan, approved by Westminster City Council in 2011, was subject to energetic debate and public scrutiny. Developed by architects Squire & Partners and Dixon Jones, with landscape designer Kim Wilkie, it reflects a move away from modernist planning principles to a more sensitive, contextual and contemporary approach. This approach emphasises continuity as an essential cultural desideratum. It is perhaps best seen as stemming from a respect for the traditions of this part of the city, and an understanding of the structure and historic patterns of the urban grain as a kind of palimpsest, which reveals a layering of traces of its past and can meaningfully inform future development. The masterplan sought to avoid creating an autonomous, impermeable luxury housing enclave. Instead, the goal was to make, as Michael Squire optimistically put it, just "another part of the city". This was to be accomplished by reknitting the site of the former barracks and parade ground into the adjacent urban fabric of streets and gardens, through reference to the characteristic London precedent of the residential garden square and terrace. The buildings enclosing the new squares are mainly 8-storey terrace-like apartment blocks along the front of the development, with lower townhouse terraces with individual gardens near where the periphery of the site meets similar existing conditions. Stylistically, the challenge was to find an expression sympathetic and comparable to – but in no way mimicking – the historic architecture of the area. The ambition and budget of the developer Qatari Diar allowed for high-quality materials, detailing and craftsmanship to be used throughout.

Eric Parry Architects' complex and subtle design is highly attuned to each building's position in the order of the whole. The masterplan has been careful to preserve and integrate pre-existing features, such as the Victorian Garrison Chapel. Traces of the Westbourne river, which once ran through this area and gave it its special character, have been reawakened in Gustafson Porter + Bowman's handsome landscaping and numerous water features. Such historical fragments, together with reimagined old local place names, were seen as a valuable source of historic continuity and collective memory.

The practice's three apartment blocks have handsome stone-built façades, evocative of the classical architectural legacy but reinterpreted in a contemporary idiom, and follow the hierarchy of the overall plan. Chelsea Bridge Road, the primary street frontage of the development and marked by the restored, listed cast-iron railings, is edged by the most formal of the three, Building 7. It sits beside and communicates along the new linear park of Bourne Walk with the Phase 1 buildings, which share the same classical tripartite structure of base, body and attic level. The practice's design complements the architectural character and materiality of the earlier phases, while also introducing new and distinct features and materials. This strategy aims at providing some heterogeneity within the development. Having self-supporting ashlar masonry façades, Building 7 faces the street with an imposing double-height

stone colonnade, with fine columns and an ornamental entablature. Building 6, forming most of the western edge along Mulberry Square, the main pedestrian axis through the development, is also entirely ashlar-clad. Building 8, which faces onto Five Fields Square, combines stone at the base and attic levels with a body of high-quality dark brickwork, evocative of Georgian and Victorian precedents, and also of the materiality of Wren's nearby Royal Hospital. Above the parapet, metal-clad duplex penthouses stand behind sculptural pergolas. The stonework throughout is of large-format Portuguese limestone, which has a slightly creamier colour and greater consistency than the Portland stone used in Phases 1 and 2. Varying groupings of recessed and projecting balconies, often with ornamental cast-metal balustrades, were a major means of articulating the façades, while adding to the apartments' amenities.

The U-shaped group of the Phase 4 buildings is partly enclosed at the northern side by the restored Garrison chapel. This Grade II-listed building is (together with the iron railings on Chelsea Barracks Road) the only structure remaining of the original Victorian barracks. It contains a war memorial and is thus of civic significance. A similar role is played by St Barnabas' Church to the north-east. Through the view of its spire, it is hoped that the new development will gain a sense of continuity as a village-like community. The chapel is now enclosed within the new pedestrian square, edged by new low-rise, mixed-use

left: View of Chelsea Hospital from the top of Eric Parry Architects' Chelsea Barracks' Building 7.

above: Chelsea Hospital's Main Court as seen from under the colonnade adjacent to the Great Hall.

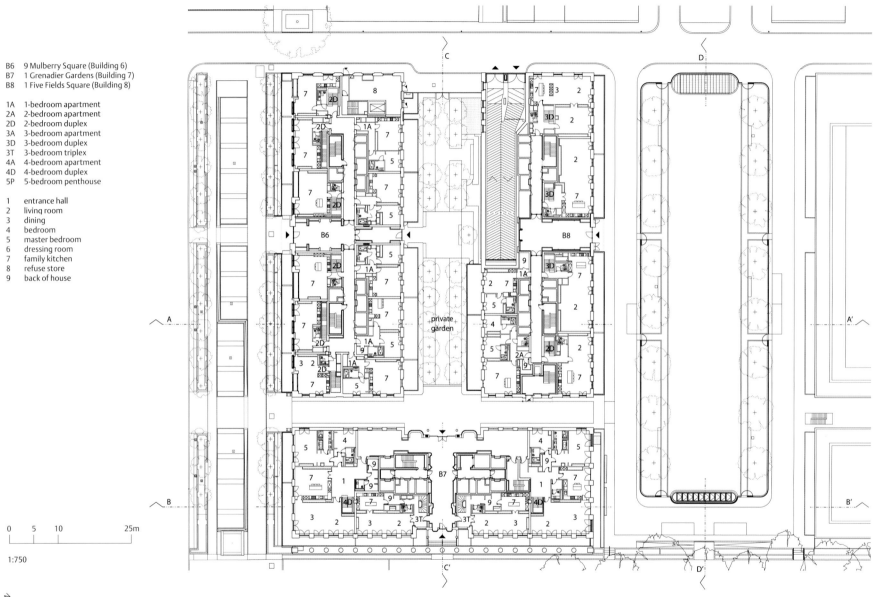

B6   9 Mulberry Square (Building 6)
B7   1 Grenadier Gardens (Building 7)
B8   1 Five Fields Square (Building 8)

1A   1-bedroom apartment
2A   2-bedroom apartment
2D   2-bedroom duplex
3A   3-bedroom apartment
3D   3-bedroom duplex
3T   3-bedroom triplex
4A   4-bedroom apartment
4D   4-bedroom duplex
5P   5-bedroom penthouse

1   entrance hall
2   living room
3   dining
4   bedroom
5   master bedroom
6   dressing room
7   family kitchen
8   refuse store
9   back of house

0   5   10   25m

1:750

N

ground floor

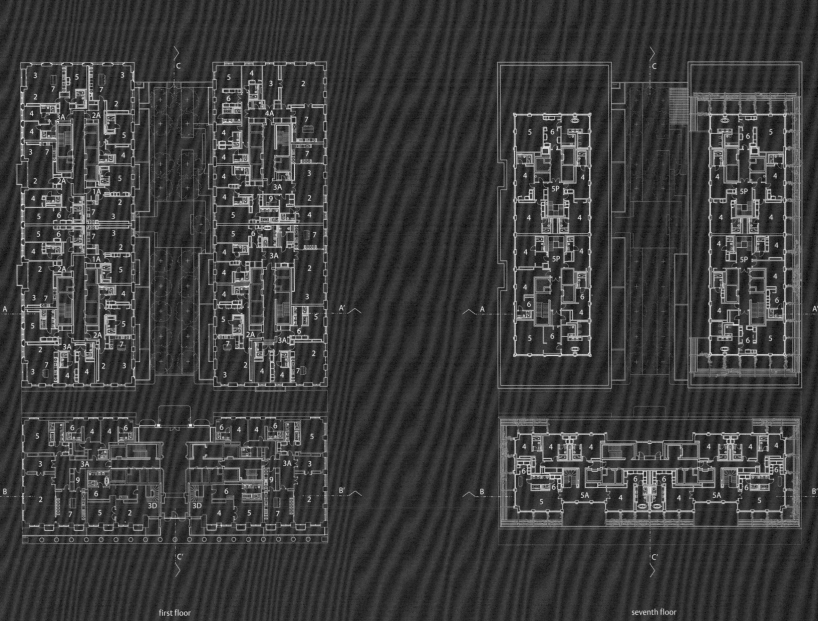

first floor

seventh floor

The first floor residence of
1 Grenadier Gardens with a view
of the colonnade and landscape.
The column shafts were initially
designed to be fluted as shown
in this visualisation produced at
competition stage.

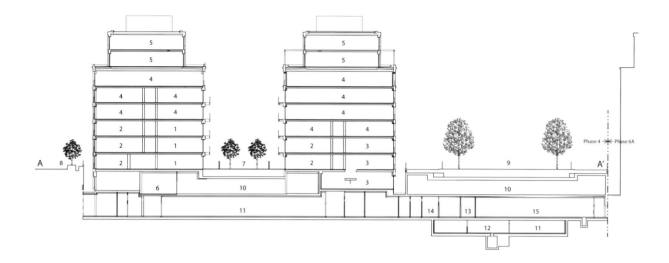

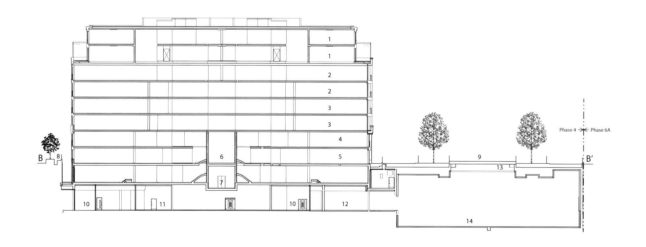

0   5   10   25m

1:750

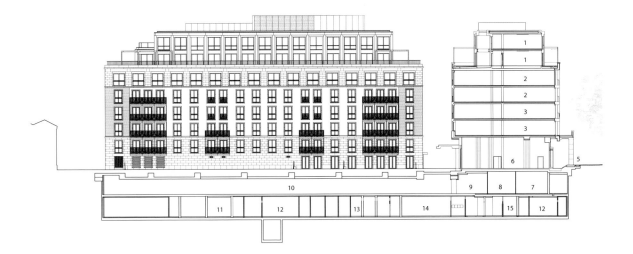

buildings. One of these, designed by Ben Pentreath, has a handsome brick arcade with shallow domes, referencing the nearby architecture of Sir John Soane, and specifically his (now destroyed) infirmary and the extant brick service buildings beside the Royal Hospital. Garrison Square's central location on Ranelagh Grove provides an opportunity for a natural social and cultural hub for the whole site. The western boundary of Chelsea Bridge Road, linking the development with the Royal Hospital, is seen as its formal entry and urban face, while buildings are positioned and ordered in such a way as to avoid uncomfortable collisions between the public and private domains.

The masterplan also stressed that there be mutually harmonious relationships between all the development's parts. This is evident in the coherent palette of materials specified by the design code: chiefly pale limestone masonry, accented with bronze-coloured metal for the penthouses and balcony balustrades. These features create a family resemblance for all the residential architecture on the estate. At the same time, differences in massing, articulation and ornamentation of the façades promote individuality and visual variety. A richness of detail was to go hand in hand with a high quality of crafting and tectonic execution to reflect the exclusivity of the estate. While stone alone is not the predominant building material in the area, it was chosen here as the main external material of the estate to suggest a sense of solidity and permanence.

The three buildings of Phase 4 are eight-storey apartment blocks based loosely on the residential terrace type. The practice cites the grand terraces which John Nash built around Regent's Park as significant precedents. These were typically blocks of large individual townhouses, built sometimes by different contractors at slightly different times, and grouped behind a unified, palatial façade. They were typically characterised by a strong tripartite order of base, body and attic, and often articulated by features such as projecting central or corner pavilions, pediments and colonnades. A common and successful feature of the great London estates' land development programme, this type can create a good density and comfortable relationships between the public and the private.

All three buildings have a concrete-frame internal structure, which supports either thick limestone ashlar or brickwork cladding, or is recessed behind an entirely self-supporting stone façade. The cream colour of the limestone and dark grey of the brickwork are complemented by the bronze and dark-coloured finishes of the metal elements. The two-storey penthouses set back on levels 6 and 7 are visually distinguished by their bronze anodised-finish cladding. The setback reduces the visual bulk of the street wall and improves light penetration to the surrounding external spaces, while providing generous roof terraces. The heavy metal pergolas of Buildings 7 and 8 provide amenity to the penthouses and articulate the setback transition. They will soon be laden with wisteria.

left: Southwest facing porch and load-bearing stone colonnade of 1 Grenadier Gardens (Building 7). The entablature contains a poem by Pelé Cox in the sculpted frieze, which constitutes possibly the longest building inscription in the West; behind it, the residential floors rise up on stone cladded piers to culminate in the pergola on the 6th floor.

above: View of the stone-clad piers during construction in March 2020.

above: Early competition study for the southwest façade of 1 Grenadier Gardens (Building 7) with the frieze initially alluding to the Panathenaic procession, a recurring motif of classical architecture.

right: Detail of the balconies to the residential floors above.

As a non-arbitrary way of creating variety, the three Phase 4 buildings differ depending on their respective roles in the hierarchy of the plan. Building 7 is situated in the centre of the Chelsea Bridge Road frontage, and will, together with the later Building 19, frame the opening to Five Fields Square. With its central location, south-west orientation and uninterrupted views, it has been seen as the most prestigious apartment building of the whole estate. To reflect this primary significance, the principal elevation has been designed as the most honorific, facing the street frontage with a grand stone colonnade. This is a civic gesture, reflecting the scale and high status of the whole of the Chelsea Barracks development. It also serves to ground the building and to emphasise its tripartite vertical order. The colonnade's monumental limestone columns are smooth, with no capitals, and are refined with perceptible entasis. They support a deep stone entablature, which serves as a balustrade to the terrace above. It carries a sculptural frieze which encircles the whole building and is inscribed with a site-specific calligraphic artwork. It had initially been proposed for the frieze to be carved in high relief with a procession of horses, according to designs by Eric Parry. This would have been a reference to the equestrian themes of the classical and royal traditions, and to the culture of the clients. Parry's conception for the equestrian frieze had been inspired by Eadweard Muybridge's photographic studies of horses in motion. At the same time, his sketches recall the reliefs of the Panathenaic procession on the Parthenon frieze.

They show a group of horses standing frontally in the middle of the colonnade over the Chelsea Bridge Road entrance, then turning and galloping in opposite directions around the building and meeting again over the vehicular drop-off on the northern side. The frontal grouping on the principal façade would also have been reminiscent of the triumphal horses of St Mark. Naturally suited to a linear format, the processional theme would have added a sense of movement to the building's girdle. Due to time pressures, the decision was eventually made to commission instead the poet Pelé Cox to create site-specific poetry for the frieze. Her free-verse poems in an elegant typeface, carved into the stone frieze in three-line clusters, appear around the building. They are themed around motifs of neighbouring Chelsea: trees, birds, gardens, poetry and the river. The laudatory inscriptions provide subtle ornamentation to the façades and lend individuality to the apartments, while recalling classical precedents. The two-layer façade above the colonnade is animated by glass-fronted balconies with cast-aluminium top rails which – in a touch of an Art Nouveau spirit – resemble swirling knots or vegetal tendrils.

Building 8 forms most of the western edge to Five Fields Square. Its two-storey stone base establishes continuity with the colonnade and piers of Building 7. Above this, the main wall up to Level 5 is made of brickwork with stone-framed windows. Four projecting blocks of deep balconies break up and give a rhythm to the long façade.

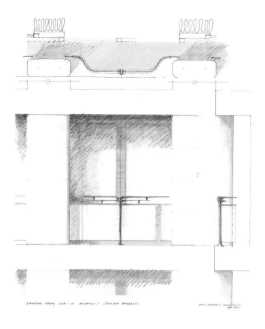

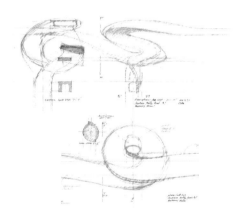

above: Early study by Eric Parry
for the fenestration of 1 Grenadier
Gardens (Building 7) already
anticipating a bespoke design
for the parapet.

below: Hand-drawn study by
Eric Parry for the hand rail to
the parapets above.

right: The completed balconies,
here in the northwestern façade
of 1 Grenadier Gardens with its
distinctive frieze poem.

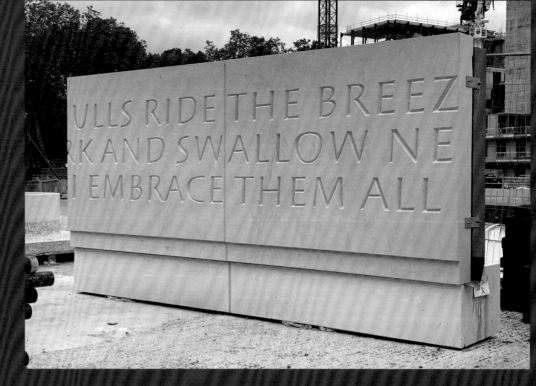

ULLS RIDE THE BREEZ
RK AND SWALLOW NE
I EMBRACE THEM ALL

top left: Stonework for
the lintels of the façade,
incorporating the outline
of the clear glass parapets.

top right: Detail of the frieze
poem by Pelé Cox.

bottom right: A column drum
base for the colonnade along
the southwestern façade of
1 Grenadier Gardens, allowing
for a site-poured concrete core
for stability and connection into
the ground structure. Above it,
the entire length of the column
shafts was built with solid stone.

As with historical prototypes, the balcony fronts enliven the façade with the ornament of their sculptural cast-aluminium balustrades, which here also recall Art Nouveau foliate motifs. The remaining windows have Juliet balconies. Level 5 is a continuous attic with stone reintroduced around larger, deep windows with shallow balconies. The penthouse levels follow the treatment at Building 7, with pergolas at the terrace level. The refined charcoal-coloured brick is used here in conjunction with the limestone and dark metalwork in reference to the characteristic London brick terraces. It creates connections with the materiality characteristic of Chelsea, and adds heterogeneity to the estate.

The main façade of Building 6 forms one of the edges of Mulberry Square. It is less formal than that of Building 8 and responds to the differing scales of the neighbouring structures, including the townhouses and chapel. To reduce the building's apparent bulk and length, two full-height recesses have been carved out of the front elevation, dividing it into three smaller blocks. This may be seen as a contemporary allusion to the tripartite massing of the neoclassical terrace. These recessed bays hold deep projecting balconies with substantial stone balustrades. The other windows of the body of the building have Juliet balconies. Each window is framed within a rebated rectangular surround panel, set slightly behind the front plane. The resulting reveals, characteristic of

Parry's recessive stone façades, create dramatic shadow rhythms and a satisfying sense of depth.

The attic level on this façade is demarcated by the different rhythm of its fenestration with deeper reveals. The corner bays are somewhat wider and equipped with shallow recessed balconies behind triple openings. Here the concave space of the corner-bay balcony may be seen as gentle subversion of the classical tradition of more solid or projecting end pavilions, while also suggesting the columnar screens which sometimes embellish them. All the openings of the facade are supported by full-width stone lintels. The external material palette of Building 6 consists only of limestone and coated metalwork. Owing perhaps to its position overlooking a major cultivated garden, Building 6 does not have the penthouse pergolas. As in Building 8, the ashlar stonework is continued into the rear elevation to the private garden. Compared to the fluted pilasters and stylised 'rustication' of the Phase 1 block across the street, Parry's classical allusions here are more nuanced and contemporary.

Five Fields Square, designed by Gustafson Porter in consultation with Eric Parry Architects, contains two avenues of trees defining a wide central lawn. Its name, which goes back here to the Middle Ages, conjures up the erstwhile rural character of this area. The square does not open directly to Chelsea Bridge Road, with Bourne Walk running

left: Early competition study for the southeastern façade of 1 Five Fields Square (Building 8), whose metal balconies are an art nouveau reference overlooking the square.

above: Hand-drawn study by Eric Parry for the metal parapet of 1 Five Fields Square.

opposite, right: View of the southeastern façade of 1 Five Fields Square.

opposite, left: Detail of one of the balconies.

uninterrupted on its south-western edge. It was envisioned as a large, multipurpose green field, to be used by residents and visitors for a variety of leisure activities, including sports and art exhibitions. It sits over the underground car park and sports centre which extend under all of Phase 4. The treatment of the surfaces and parking around the square is aimed at attracting wider community use.

The two subterranean levels of Phase 4 contain residents' parking and storage and a sumptuous private members' sports club with well-appointed spa facilities and a 25m pool. There is a wealth of engaging, richly tactile finishes in the sports centre and spa, including travertine, hand-made tiles, much fine joinery, fabric panelling and leather. The triple-height skylit sports hall, situated under the southern portion of Five Fields Square, has a fritted-glass sports floor with an LED lighting system which differentiates it for various activities.

As might be expected for such a prestigious project, where an aura of expensiveness was one of the requisite qualities, the Phase 4 buildings manifest a very high quality of materials and handcraft. This is obviously true of the ashlar stonework. All meticulously formed and laid with consistent, narrow lime mortar joints, it was designed with deep reveals to evoke the solidity of traditional stone construction. It is true also of the mellow brickwork on Building 8, detailed in such a way as to make the necessary movement joints almost invisible.

The many different window assemblies have all been carefully tested in full-scale mock-ups to ensure comfort of use and sophistication of appearance. The different types of cast-metal balustrades – the orthogonal Juliet balconies, the serpentine curves, the foliate motifs – each has its own elegant detailing. The curved glass balconies with the coiling 'knot' top rails on the double façades of Building 7 are a good example of this, as the convex curves of the glass panels are echoed below by the undulating outline of the granite pavers recessed tightly into the polished precast lintels. The grey granite, used throughout the development as external paving and to articulate the transition between the buildings and the earth, turns up to create a base to the limestone columns of the colonnade.

One of the most interesting aspects of Chelsea Barracks' Phase 4 is the subtle and inventive ways in which the buildings meaningfully relate to each other and to the other nearby blocks, streets and squares. As each façade responds to its specific situation within the cluster, there is a recognition of the importance of the relationships within the urban order. The high-spec ornamental embellishments integral to the architecture are designed to enhance the shared, publicly accessible outdoor spaces. The style of the architecture is informed by an understanding of the themes of the classical tradition, but these have been reinvented to accord with contemporary needs and construction techniques.

MY FLINT EYES SPARK AND DART   MY CABBAGE FACE AND MUSHROOM LIPS   THE FIRST POET MADE A ROOF OF STARS   ON THE LAWNS WARRIORS DREAM
IN THE SINKHOLES OF THE RAIN   TWIST ROUND STUMP AND BRANCHING TRUNK   MY ELMS ARE PILLARS   PUT DOWN THEIR ARMS
UNDER LICHEN HOLLOW AND IVY MANE   WAKING I LIFT ACHING LIMBS TO CROWN   MY PLANES ARE MASTS   ALL AT EASE IN THIS TEMPLE OF PEACE

On the façade, the inscribed text reads (across panels):

BREEZE ... BOUQUETS OF STARLINGS DARKLY ... ALONG THE POOLED MAZE ... ALONG THIS RIVER ROAD ... SWEEP ALONG THE SKY
... NEST THEIR MURMUROUS COIL ... I SWEETEN THE EMBALMED EARTH ... I FIND MYSELF IN OTHER BODY ... THESE VAST SHOULDERS THE ...
M ALL IN ELLIPSES OF MEMORY ... PAST WORMS BONES AND CLAY ... MY BRONZE GREEN BEARD AND FLOWING LOCKS ... ABOVE ME RUN THE HI ...

General view of the façade
of 1 Grenadier Gardens.

1 Undershaft

In thinking about tall buildings, Parry notes the role such structures have always played in the identity and collective memory of cities. Placing a tower in the middle of a grouping of diverse shapes called for a calm and elegant form. Its design was developed through a series of logical steps. The aim was to create a simple, muscular and legible structure with a multivalent, functional envelope. Its height of 294m was determined in consultation with the Civil Aviation Authority.

1 Undershaft is Eric Parry Architects' first skyscraper, and a new chapter in the practice's ongoing explorations into the nature of the contemporary urban workplace. Following an invited competition, the project received planning consent in 2016. It comprises an enlarged new public square surmounted by an office tower which rises to 304.94m AOD to crown the Eastern High-rise Cluster in the City of London's financial district. Skyscrapers have sometimes been seen as form-fixated embodiments of corporate greed, indifferent or even harmful to the historic fabric and microclimate of the city. To counter these criticisms, the practice took great care with the design of the street-level domain from which the tower rises, so that it enhances the qualities of civic life for workers and local residents.

The building site at St Helen's Square is circumscribed by St Mary Axe to the east, the Undershaft – the road which gives the building its name – to the north and the Leadenhall Building to the west. It is presently occupied by St Helen's Aviva Tower (reclad after it suffered bomb damage in the 1990s), which limits visibility and pedestrian flow with its impermeable ground floor. The precise location of the new tower was informed by a thorough consideration of all the protected views of St Paul's Cathedral, as well as the need for the high-rise cluster to have a central focus. The existing square has been enlarged on the north side by the removal of an obstructive service ramp and by a

slight shift of the road layout. The tower stands on the northern half of a new square. It is arranged around the dramatic feature of an almost completely open ground-level base, which leaves the area underneath the building accessible to pedestrian movement and facilitates cross views from all directions. The new square also brings together a pair of somewhat marooned medieval city churches of St Helen Bishopsgate and St Andrew Undershaft (giving them enhanced recognition and more breathing space) and the listed Lloyd's Building. The public realm here thus becomes an even more evocative collage of the old and new. It occupies the sunnier, southern part of the site and is made fully accessible by the removal of the existing peripheral stairs. At its centre is a large oval sunken court, which allows natural light into the 1800m² lower-ground retail gallery and opens up vertiginous views of the tower from below. Scaled so as to provide protection from the winds which often buffet the area, the court is lined by cafés, restaurants and shops. They look out onto the elliptical event space which in winter can become a skating rink. The lower ground levels occupy the largely retained existing basement, minimising the need for new excavations into virgin ground. They contain the plant and services, disabled car parking spaces and storage facilities for at least 1,700 bicycles. This court, with its sweeping staircases, bike ramp and seating, is somewhat reminiscent of an antique arena and will act as a theatrical urban forum. Parry has written about the sunken court of the Rockefeller Center as a

above: Competition sketch by Eric Parry showing the initial concept for 1 Undershaft as a central marker around which the remainder of the future cluster of buildings would be organised.

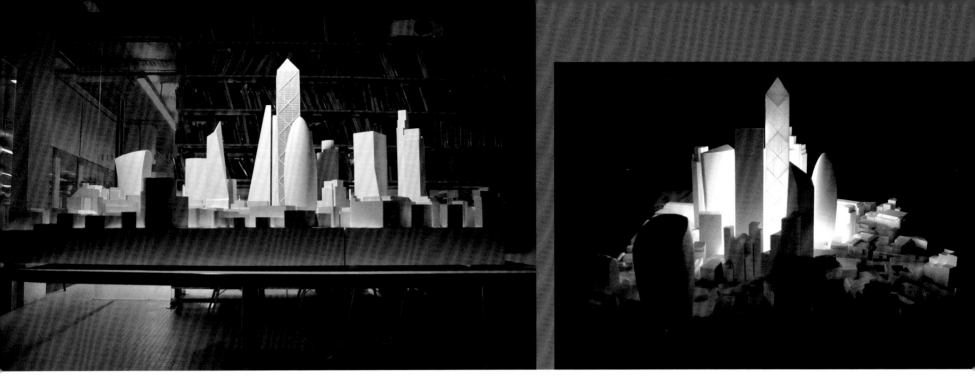

highly successful urban precedent, and some of its influence is evident in this design. The Undershaft court also recalls the ceremonial oval staircase of the practice's recently completed Leathersellers' Seventh Hall in St Helen's Place, which similarly transformed a subterranean domain with a striking architectural feature.

The space below the tower is generously proportioned, with a total height of 18m (10m to the underside of the reception level soffit), and offers the opportunity for a newly commissioned public art installation. From it, escalators provide access to the raised office reception hall. As planting struggles to flourish in some parts of the Cluster, the new square will contain mostly high-quality hard landscaping, with trees concentrated on the sunniest, south side of the site.

In thinking about tall buildings, Parry notes the role such structures have always played in the identity and collective memory of cities. Placing a tower in the middle of a grouping of diverse shapes called for a calm and elegant form. Its design was developed through a series of logical steps. The aim was to create a simple, muscular and legible structure with a multivalent, functional envelope. Its height of 294m was determined in consultation with the Civil Aviation Authority. Given the configuration and constraints of the site, a decision was taken to place an offset core, containing the many lifts required for a

building of this height, on the western side of the structure, adjacent to that of the Leadenhall Building. Side servicing via vehicle lifts to an underground loading bay results in the core having a minimum presence at ground level. This creates an efficient office floor plate and works in tandem with the exoskeleton of weathering steel cross braces, connected to the perimeter columns (as major and minor picture frames), to provide the requisite stiffness. The office floor plan is approximately $45m^2$, with four piers at the centre and an efficiently sized structural bay of 13.5m. The stem of the building is divided into three vertical groupings of 12 floors with four groupings of 10 floors above. The glass skin between the cross-bracing is veiled by an outer layer of white vitreous-enamel brise-soleil, which provide a good level of defence against solar gain and create a shadow rhythm on the façade. This durable material also gives the tower a luminous, whitish appearance, contrasting with the dull green tinge of many City glass curtain walls. The colour and patina of the weathering steel will vary with time, orientation and environmental conditions, and will give the building a rich texture. This treatment also animates the elevations with a play of shadow and light, adding visual depth.

The tower's profile is refined by the classical technique of entasis. Parry cites the entasis of Edwin Lutyens' Cenotaph in Whitehall, the dignified monument in which both the stone stylobate and blade

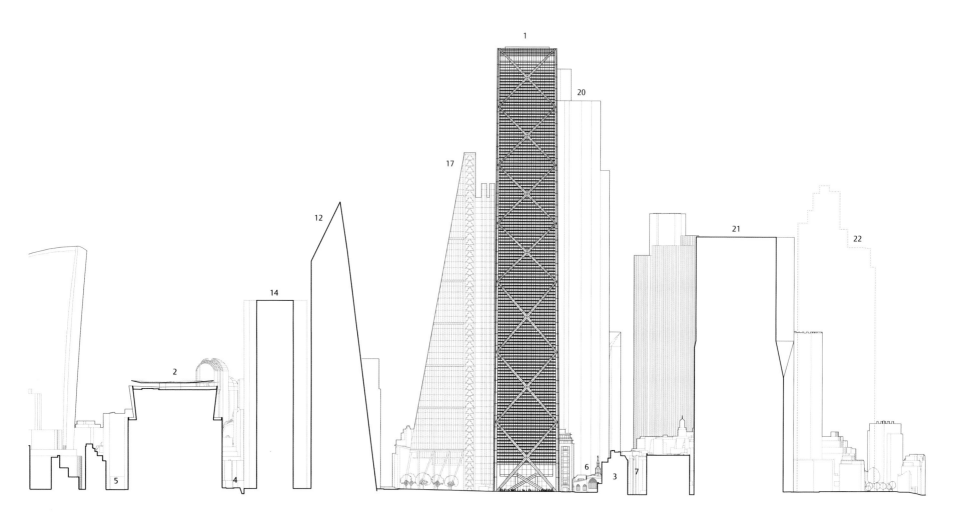

location section

1:2500

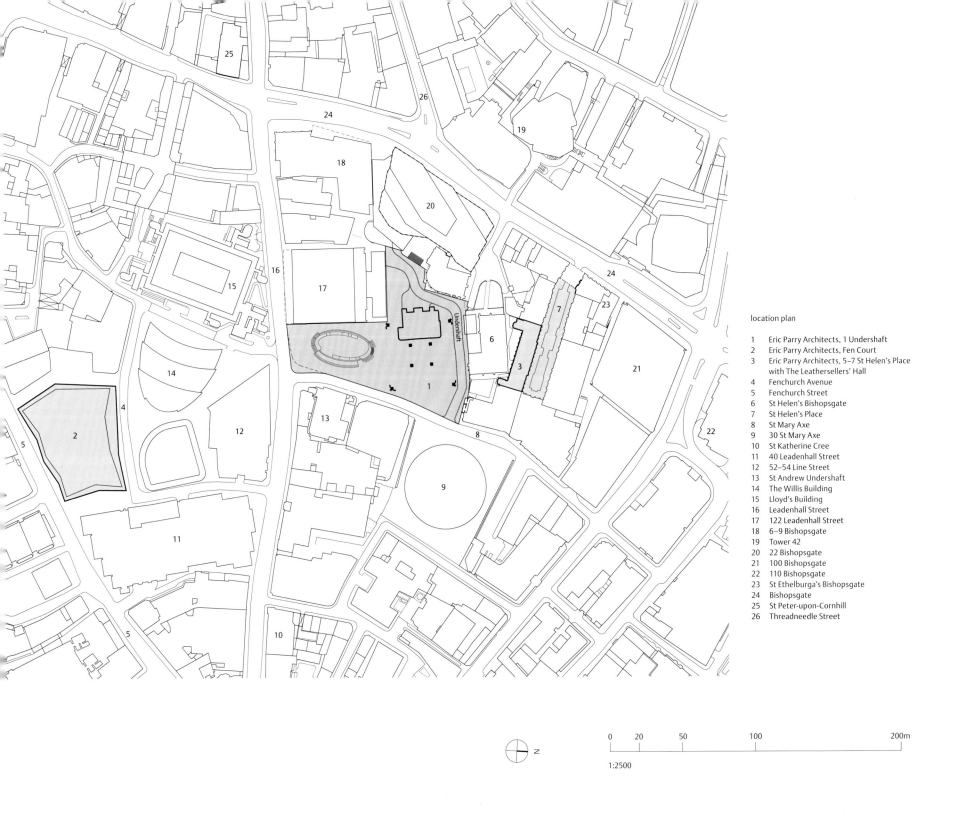

location plan

1   Eric Parry Architects, 1 Undershaft
2   Eric Parry Architects, Fen Court
3   Eric Parry Architects, 5–7 St Helen's Place
    with The Leathersellers' Hall
4   Fenchurch Avenue
5   Fenchurch Street
6   St Helen's Bishopsgate
7   St Helen's Place
8   St Mary Axe
9   30 St Mary Axe
10 St Katherine Cree
11 40 Leadenhall Street
12 52–54 Line Street
13 St Andrew Undershaft
14 The Willis Building
15 Lloyd's Building
16 Leadenhall Street
17 122 Leadenhall Street
18 6–9 Bishopsgate
19 Tower 42
20 22 Bishopsgate
21 100 Bishopsgate
22 110 Bishopsgate
23 St Ethelburga's Bishopsgate
24 Bishopsgate
25 St Peter-upon-Cornhill
26 Threadneedle Street

0   20   50   100   200m

1:2500

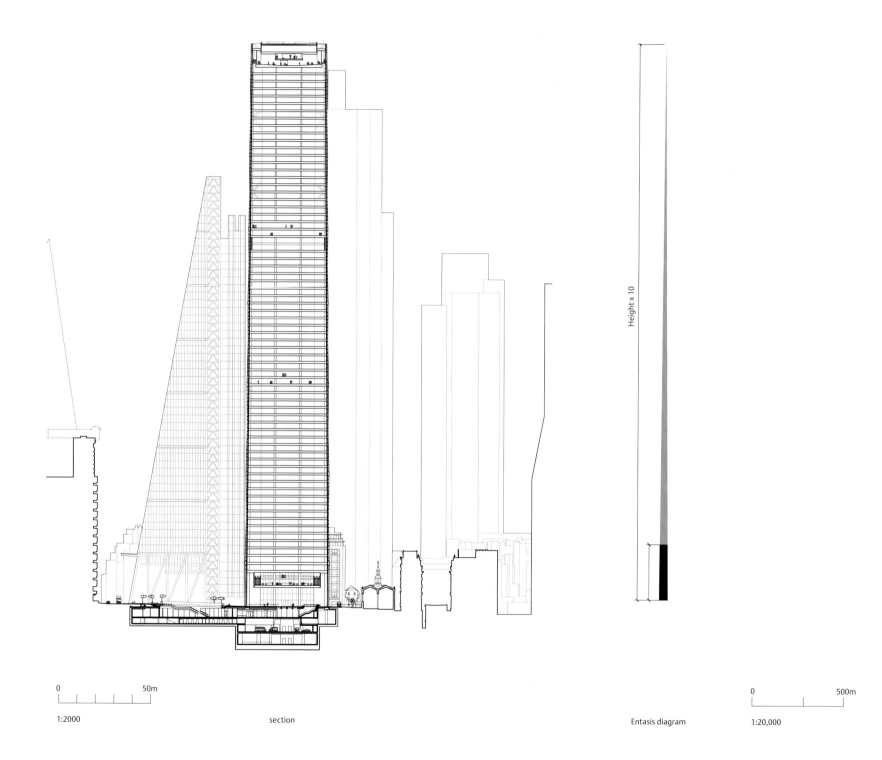

0   50m

1:2000   section

Height x 10

0   500m

Entasis diagram   1:20,000

left and right: Visualisations of the new square from ground level and the lower ground, looking towards 1 Undershaft.

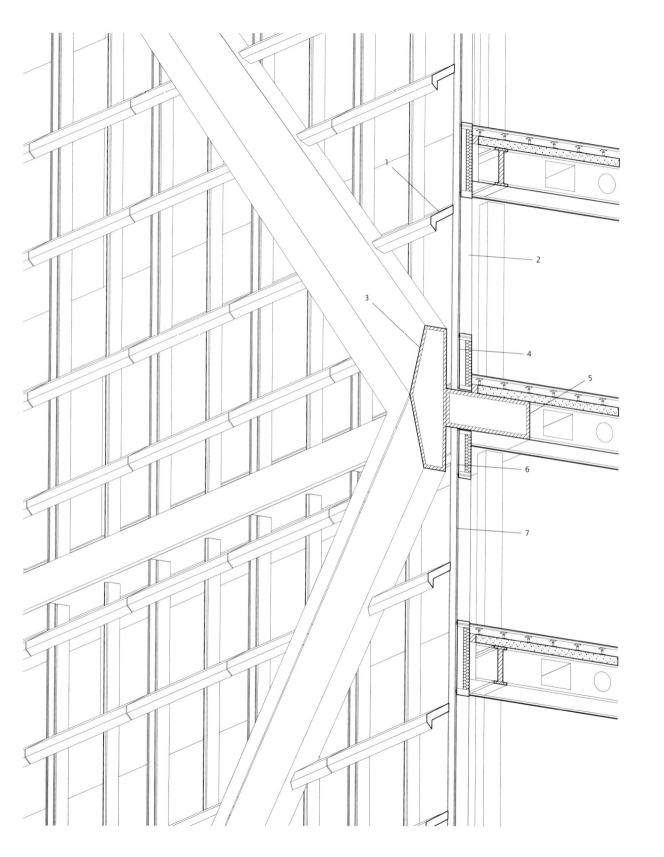

axonometric section

1 brise-soleil with white vitreous enamel finish
2 aluminium insulated curtain walling
3 weathering steel
4 spandrel-panel, behind external bracing
5 structural node connection
6 glazed spandrel-panel with white frit to low-iron glass
7 double-glazed unit, low-iron glass

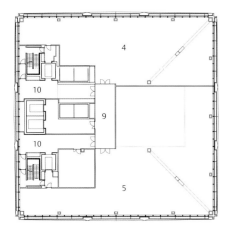

public restaurant / amenity (level 70)

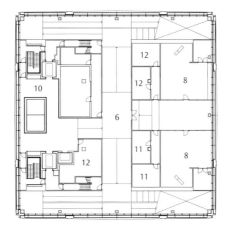

viewing gallery arrival / education space (level 71)

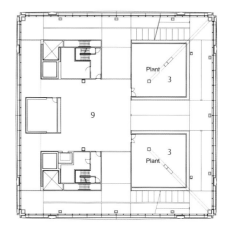

viewing gallery upper level (level 72)

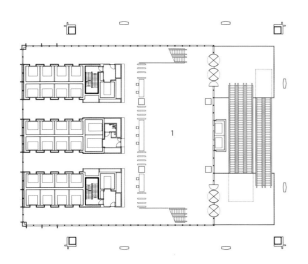

level 01 office reception lower level

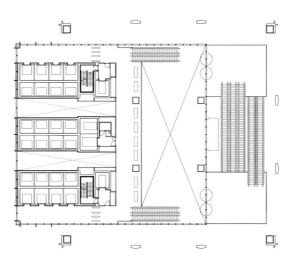

level 02 office reception upper level

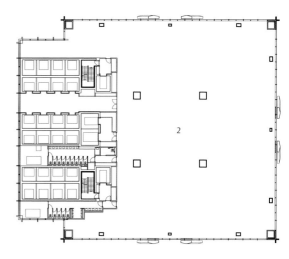

level 03 office

1   reception
2   office
3   plant
4   office restaurant
5   public restaurant
6   viewing gallery
7   classroom
8   restaurant lobby
9   upper viewing gallery
10 lift lobby
11 cloakroom
12 wc

N

0   10   20m

1:750

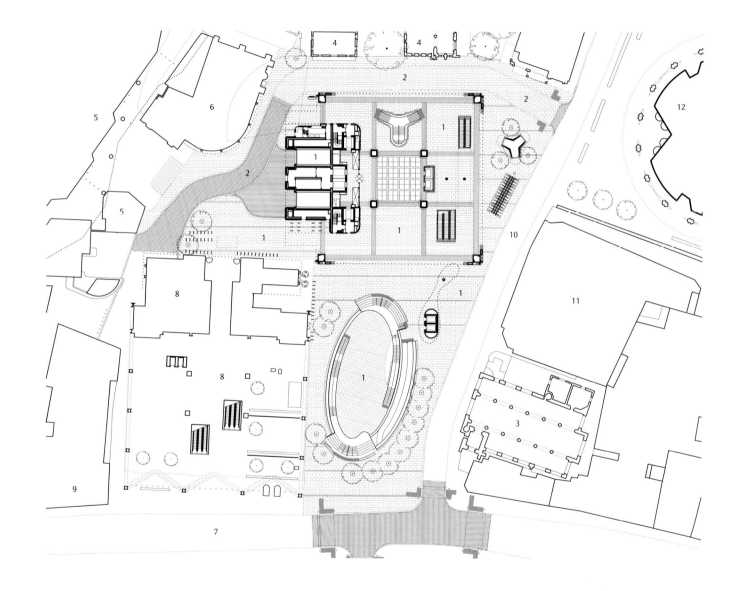

ground plan

1   Eric Parry Architects, 1 Undershaft
2   Undershaft
3   St Andrew's Undershaft
4   St Helen's Bishopsgate
5   22 Bishopsgate
6   1 Great St Helen's
7   Leadenhall Street
8   122 Leadenhall Street
9   140 Leadenhall Street
10 St Mary Axe
11 Fitzwilliam House
12 30 St Mary Axe

N

0   10   25   50m

1:1000

above: View of the model for the new square allowing for a permeable public realm at ground level, here seen from the east.

0 1   5   10m

1:400

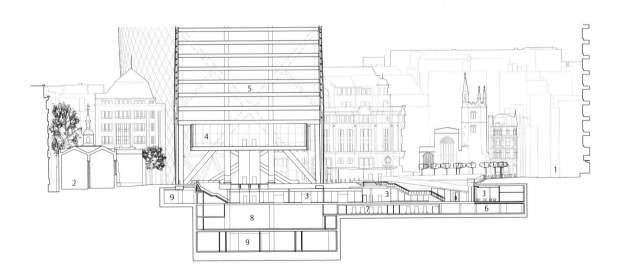

eastward section through public realm and basements

1   Leadenhall Street
2   St Helen's Church Bishopsgate
3   retail
4   reception / lift transfer floor
5   office
6   cycle parking
7   cycle amenity
8   loading
9   plant room

0   10   25   50m

1:1000

have been built with a barely perceptible convex curvature, refining the structure's appearance and creating a symbolic connection – appropriate to a war memorial – between the earth and heaven. In a similar way, the Undershaft's sides are subtly adjusted, its entasis arrived at by projecting the vertical outlines of the 294m-high tower upward, so that they eventually converge at ten times the building's height, that is at 2,940m above London. The structural elements and the tower itself grow more slender as they rise. This makes pragmatic sense while also improving the tower's appearance and dramatising its sense of ascent. The building will contain approximately 90,000m² of office space, its slight taper resulting also in a commercially useful variation in the size of the floor plates.

Parry's precedents for the tower inform the design. He admires the simple beauty of the pragmatic, engineering structures of early twentieth-century industrial architecture. In the concrete cooling towers of German power stations, for example, the forms of the external bracing are dictated by the need for height and stiffness, and create a dramatic architectural effect. The slender medieval house towers in cities like Bologna are also relevant. In addition to their defensive function, these varied structures proclaimed the patrician families' identity and standing in the civic community.

The vertically accented cap of the tower relates to the sky and offers civic amenities. Its three levels contain UK's highest public viewing gallery, served by dedicated lifts, with a public restaurant located on the level below. In an unusual twist, this part of the building also contains a free educational component, run in conjunction with the Museum of London. Here the intention is that parties of schoolchildren, brough up by the dedicated lifts, are able to learn about the evolving history of London by looking through an animated cyclorama superimposed over the dramatic present-day views of the city. This is another instance of Parry deploying an inventive, views-linked visual device, whose roots go back to the novel optical technologies and simulated realities which were all the rage in the European cities of the early nineteenth century. It illustrates the highly imaginative, civically minded use of the building's great height.

Projects summary

Lipton Residence II

In summer 2009 the approval for the reconstruction of this 1930s house, which we had already extensively remodelled (see *Volume 1*), was granted. Two immediate neighbours had already been rebuilt as neo-Georgian facsimiles, but ours was to be a contemporary version of the Regency villa. The commission was for a lifetime family home that would demonstrate sustainable construction and achieve Code for Sustainable Homes Level 4. The level access allowed a section and massing with three full floors above ground with an enlarged lower ground floor. The street elevation has a suppressed and heavily glazed ground floor with ten portrait format windows to the bedrooms above. To the garden are the more expressive volumes of the principal rooms. The garden has been designed by Adriaan Geuze of West 8. The interiors were in collaboration with Chester Jones and developed the vocabulary of the original design, this time incorporating and articulating the reused elements. The landscaped garden, terraces and retained fish pool were completed with West 8.

C: Sir Stuart and Lady Ruth Lipton
SE: Arup
M&E: Arup
QS: Davis Langdon
LA: West 8 (Rotterdam)
Interior designer: Chester Jones Ltd
A: EP, RK, RD, DL, ZF, RLL, BL
Date: 2007–2012

St John's Waterloo

We were commissioned in 2010 to undertake a feasibility study on the entire site and find how its currently underused building and churchyard could best be used for the local community. A masterplan included a dramatically improved worship space, better connectivity to the Crypt which was re-arranged to provide more community uses, plus new below ground facilities including a double-height Community Hall and Chapel. A Community Café stands as a pavilion in the Churchyard. This first phase is contained within the existing footprint of the Church and sought to improve accessibility and use of the Church and Crypt. The intention was to return to the Georgian clarity of the entrance sequence and enable a clear line of sight from outside the Church into the east end. We proposed a generous entrance area, with a new lift and a stair within a foyer created by a glazed screen under the west gallery. New galleries were proposed in the Church to mediate natural light and lead the eye to the east end as well as increase the capacity and afford opportunities for greater choral and theatrical uses of the Church.

C: The Parish of St John with St Andrew Waterloo
SE: Alan Baxter
Acoustic engineer: Gillieron Scott
M&E: Skelly & Couch
QS: Academy Consulting
A: EP, TL, PBA, CD, JM, KS
Date: 2010–ongoing

Fen Court

Fen Court is a development at the scale of a city block. Following a transfer of ownership, the initial scheme from 2007 was revised and received approval. It retains three distinct sections: a permeable base with a new public passageway; a main body of nine storeys of high-quality office space; and an upper setback with four office floors with a restaurant and a publicly accessible roof garden above. The specific geometry of the site informed the strong, facetted massing. The vertical, ceramic fins along with a series of horizontal brise-soleil provide depth and solar shading. The crystalline form of the upper fully glazed floors reflects the surrounding buildings and sky. The roof garden has a new topography of a gently folding landscape, a water feature and green cubes which enclose the plant facilities below. Encircling its high level 'wisteria canopy' a continuous perimeter walk gives vistas of the London skyline in all four directions. An LED screen soffit at the centre of the pedestrian passageway shows imagery of the roof garden above.

C: Generali Saxon Land Development Company
PM: Core
SE: Arup
M&E: Waterman Group
QS: Gleeds
LA: Latz + Partner
A: EP, NJ* (2), PBA* (3), RD, CT, CK, DP, PF, SP, CSL, ED, ELP, KS, CD, RL, RK* (1), DL, ARM, SF, NA, AG, TN
Date: 2006–2018

Vicarage Gate House

Vicarage Gate House is at the junction of Vicarage Gate and Palace Garden Terrace, bordering the rear of Palace Green Terrace. The main entrance to the development reception is from Vicarage Gate, with a broad landscaped courtyard to the rear. The building massing and façade respond to the existing context. The north elevation complements the neighbouring terraces with traditional masonry brickwork, horizontal precast banding, purpose-made punched windows and a zinc mansard at roof level. A ceramic bay with curved windows celebrates the complexity of the building's location. To the east, a stepped terrace provides residents with external spaces. The south elevation consists of brick piers and full-height picture windows. There are bespoke balconies that offer private amenity spaces for ease of living, in line with Code for Sustainable Homes Level 4. Planning consent was granted in February 2013. Practical completion was achieved in April 2016 with tenants taking occupation.

C: Vicarage Gate Limited
PM: Northacre
SE: Conisbee
QS: Hampton
Interior designers: Forme Architecture
Building Service Engineer: Mecserve
A: EP, JO, BD*, AM, AW, EF, ARM, SF
Date: 2011–2016

1–9 Seymour Street

The site at 1–9 Seymour Street and 6–16 Bryanston Street is owned as a freehold by The Portman Estate. A 1970s building for the Metropolitan Police Authority replaced original Georgian townhouses. It had been recently vacated as part of its consolidation programme within Central London. The property is located between Seymour Street to the north and Bryanston Street to the south. The site is within the Core Central Activities Zone, the Portman Estate Conservation Area and the Baker Street Quarter Business Improvement District. The project has two aspects: Seymour Street to the north and Bryanston Street to the south. The Portman Estate aims to redevelop with a mix of residential, retail – specifically a restaurant – and office space with replacement social and community use that provides an improved community asset in their estate and targeted to achieve BREEAM Outstanding.

C: The Portman Estate
PM: Avison Young
SE: Furness Partnership
QS: Alinea
LA: Garden Makers
A: EP, RK, LH, RC, LM, HT, KS, LB, LMB, RRP, BF, EF
Date: 2012–2018

111 Buckingham Palace Road

111 Buckingham Palace Road is part of the Over Site Development (OSD) created in the 1980s near the southwest platforms of Victoria railway station. The large office floors are above the Plaza Shopping Centre. The office entrance is on the east side of Buckingham Palace Road directly south of the Grosvenor Hotel. The office building has a long façade of mirrored glass cladding that returns onto Eccleston Bridge to the south and to the raised service and taxi court to the east side. Our proposal only concerned the ground floor office entrance and its enclosure. The brief was to improve the presence of the office building on Buckingham Palace Road as well as the tenants' and visitors' arrival experience. This was proposed by enlarging the reception and bringing it forward to enclose the forecourt. The site was originally the parcel office for the station with access from the street for vans and a frontage onto the station concourse behind; and the proposed work increased these back-of-house areas to the line of the new east wall to the reception. The removal of vehicular crossovers allowed improvements to the pavement and quality of public realm.

C: Kennedy Wilson
PM: Burnley Wilson Fish
SE: Price & Myers
M&E: Blyth and Blyth
QS: Burnley Wilson Fish and Gleeds
A: EP, RK, BD, MV, TS
Date: 2013–2016

Cambridge University Press & Assessment

We were appointed to design the new headquarters for Cambridge Assessment in 2013, following a limited competition. Established over 150 years ago, Cambridge Assessment operates and manages the University's three exam boards and carries out academic and operational research on assessment in education. Known as Cambridge University Press & Assessment from October 2020, the development provides approximately 350,000ft^2 (NIA) of new office and amenity space for 3,000 people with 1,325 bicycle spaces. Our vision was an inspiring new group of connected buildings, ranging from four to five storeys in height. These are shallow depth fingers set around raised landscaped podia with a central arrival court and garden. The façades are formed of bands of hand-set brickwork in lime mortar, combined with light coloured self-finished precast concrete elements, and include a visual arts intervention by Vong Phaophanit and Claire Oboussier. A taller tower is located along the railway, marking the site when viewed from the busway and railway approach into Cambridge station. The tower is scaled to the local context and does not compete with the existing taller landmark buildings in Cambridge. The building is highly sustainable and targeting a DEC A rating from occupation.

C: Cambridge Assessment
PM: Turner and Townsend
SE: Ramboll
M&E: Max Fordham
QS: Aecom
LA: Grant Associates
A: EP, NJ, TN, CT, EH, MJ, RP, WW, MV, CL, CRD
Date: 2013–2018

London Residence

This London property is in a Grade II* listed building within the City of Westminster Belgravia Conservation Area, originally built as part of the grand townhouses developed by Cubitt in the 1830s. We have set out to create a contemporary residence with an improved relationship to the rear garden, all the while respecting its architectural heritage. The two levels are connected via an elliptical stair, and collaboration with the lighting designer Ingo Maurer looked to define the image and experience of the approach to the staircase.

The proposed alterations to the existing structure involved removing load-bearing walls at lower ground to help create a large family room. The aim was to re-establish the elegance of the original house, whilst simultaneously maximising natural light with an extension that is sympathetic to the existing building.

C: Private Client
SE: Michael Hadi Associates
M&E: Ralph T. King & Associates
QS: Corrigan Gore & Street
LA: Arne Maynard Garden Design
A: EP, CH* (1), SF* (2), TJ, EF, JH, LO, NV
Date: 2013–2018

One Liverpool Street

Today the building at One Liverpool Street is between the ongoing infrastructure works, the excavations for the Crossrail project for Liverpool Street Station and the ventilation shaft on the adjacent Blomfield Street site. The existing building looks forlorn and is mostly emptied, but once the works are completed it will directly face the new Liverpool Street Crossrail entrance across a new public space. The Joint Venture provides the opportunity for the existing building to be demolished and replaced with an office building that through structural engineering solutions can deliver a quality and quantum of Grade A office space, not possible on the individual sites. At the heart of the financial district, our proposed office building will provide a more fitting civic backdrop to the proposed new public space and relate to the grand architecture of Liverpool Street Station. The site's proximity to the transport hub allows for further densification of commercial uses through animated frontages with both retail and office entrances and the continued improvement of the public realm.

C: Aviva
PM: WT Partnership
SE: Mott MacDonald
M&E: Aecom
QS: Gardiner & Theobald
A: EP, RK, JS, BD, MJ, CK, LM, CD, JFR, DC, JT
Date: 2013–ongoing

Carlton House Terrace

Refurbishment of Grade I-listed Regency townhouse off the Mall in central London, reworking of main stair to lower ground floor and introduction of a winter garden at ground floor level. The building was heavily damaged by bombing during WWII and later reconfigured as a home for the Royal College of Pathologists before being acquired by a financial institution. Our proposal included conference and meeting rooms with private and general office spaces, breakout spaces and a sunroom and terrace at roof level. An apartment was proposed at level 2 and a staff studio room at level 3.

C: Private Client
A: EP, RK, TS*, ASM, SO, MJ, CRD
Date: 2014–2018

1–3 Grosvenor Square

The relocation of the American Embassy and other diplomatic missions has enabled Grosvenor Square to become once again the premiere Mayfair residential square. Eric Parry Architects was appointed by Lodha UK, following an invited competition, to convert the former Canadian High Commission to residential use. After early consultations with The Grosvenor Estate and Westminster City Council, a strategy of dismantlement followed by subtly modified reconstruction of the main façades was developed; this strategy provided 44 super-prime residential units and an acoustically isolated basement, enabling protection from the Jubilee Line, housing residential amenity areas, an automated car stacker and plant rooms. The traditional façades are complemented by sympathetic contemporary and penthouse façades, a discreet arrivals court, new restaurant and a public artwork by Alison Wilding RA.

C: Lodha Group
SE: AKT II
M&E: Hoare Lea
QS & Contract Administrator: Arcadis
Façade Engineer: Arup Façades
Interior Designer: Yabu Pushelberg
Executive Architect: EPR
A: EP, RK, MC, JS, JSC, RSW, DL, AM, MIP, SP, SO, AR, VG, KB, KP, IS, ZP
Date: 2014–2020

One Chamberlain Square, Paradise Circus, Birmingham

The Masterplan for Paradise was designed by Glenn Howells Architects and received outline planning approval in February 2013. In April 2014, we were invited by the Development Manager Argent to enter an architectural competition for Building D of the approved Masterplan. We won the competition and were appointed to begin design work in September 2014. The building proposal was developed between September 2014 and June 2015 in conjunction with Argent through a rigorous design process and formal pre-application consultations with Birmingham City Council, Historic England and The Design Council.

C: Hermes Investment Management
Development Manager: Argent
PM: Faithful + Gould
SE and M&E: Arup
LA: Grant Associates
A: EP, NJ, LH, ARM, MN, RP, CRD, JIS, CB, CD, TN
Date: 2014–2019

30 St James's Square

30 St James's Square is formed by two interconnected office buildings of 21 and 22 Pall Mall, set within the St James's Conservation Area of Westminster. The proposal for 30 St James's Square comprised the retention of the existing basement, with a new core and structure constructed behind a retained façade; and extended one storey to provide six storeys above ground, with a new mansard roof concealing a roof plant room. The building includes six floors of speculative office accommodation, above the office entrance and retail on the ground floor.

The design of 30 St James's Square was driven by principles of sustainable design in order to reduce energy consumption in occupation and to provide a comfortable and healthy environment for its users. The building achieves a BREEAM "Excellent" rating.

C: Knight Frank
Development Manager: Hanover Cube
SE: Price & Myers
M&E: KJ Tait Engineers
QS: Quantem Consulting LLP
A: EP, RD, MM, RP, FW, MV, JT, WA
Date: 2015–2021

Chelsea Barracks

We won the competition for Phase 4 of the Chelsea Barracks site, with a high-end residential proposal including car parking, spa and sports centre. Our design consists of three new apartment buildings around a private court, and an additional area of soft landscaping. Built in stone, the façades are evocative of the British architectural legacy and its Classical references, calling upon the collaboration of Pelé Cox in the long stone frieze poem that punctuates the architecture with a new work of public art.

C: Chelsea Barracks (4) GP LLP
PM: WYG
SE: Arup
M&E: Hoare Lea
QS: Gleeds
LA: Gustafson Porter
A: EP, RK, NJ, MC, TP, ARM, CB, TN, DL, AR, MJ, SH, AM, BL, CLK, GW, JM, JIS, KB, VG, MIP, MP, MV, RRP, SP, TA, AW, LG, EA, AG, BT, SF, ALC, EVP
Date: 2015–2021

Central Street

Feasibility study for the redevelopment of UCG's site on 31–37 Central / 63 Gee Street, comprising a '50s office building on 63 Gee Street and small scale terraced houses and a pub on 31–37 Central Street. The brief is to develop feasible options for a new mixed use building on 31–37 Central Street that connects to the existing 63 Gee Street building. The new development will feature A1/A3 use on ground and lower ground floor, with office accommodation ready for tenant use on the upper floors and a portion of residential on the top two floors. A planning application will be targeted, following an initial pre-application meeting with Islington Council.

C: Universal Consolidated Group
A: EP, JSC, CK, TS, ELP, AO, LW, TP, CT, GGP, MM, WW, AW, FW
Date: 2020–2022

1 Undershaft

A detail planning application was submitted to the City of London in January 2016 for the 73-storey development at 1 Undershaft in the City of London. At 289.94m tall, it will rise to a height of 304.94m AOD (Above Ordnance Datum), crowning the new cluster of planned skyscrapers in the Square Mile. The building will provide approximately 90,000m² of office space. The offset design of the core and the rigidity provided by the unique external bracing means floor space has been maximised providing much needed flexible, quality office accommodation for businesses in the City of London. A new larger public square will be created at the base of the tower. The elevated office reception lobby means that the public will be able to walk freely beneath the skyscraper. Retail space will be created in the lower level retail gallery, with new restaurants, cafés and shops accessed from the public square. At the top of the building will be the UK's highest public viewing gallery, served by dedicated lifts. A public restaurant will be located on the level beneath the viewing gallery.

C: Aroland Holdings Ltd and Perennial and Wilmar International Ltd
SE: WSP
Vertical transportation: WSP
Fire enginnering: WSP
QS: Aecom
A: EP, NJ, TP, SH, TN, JIS, JSC, WW CD, MN, ED
Date: 2015–ongoing

Marylebone Lane Hotel

Our proposal is to remove the existing 1970s brutalist car park in Marylebone Lane and build a high-end boutique hotel of 206 rooms. The new hotel will have two basement levels with business and fitness facilities, as well as a café, bar and signature restaurant on the ground level, fostering the improvement of the public realm. There are nine levels of accommodation above, including a members' lounge with a small pool on level 9. The concrete frame structure accommodates for arrangement of the 2.6m-clear ceiling height guestrooms around the perimeter and the central light well. The exterior is to be clad in extruded faience panels with horizontal blue banding, continuing onto the sculptural roof.

C: Shiva Hotels
PM: Buro Four
SE: Manhire Associates
M&E: Elementa Consulting
QS: Gardiner & Theobald
A: EP, NJ, CB, EF, KB, EVP, KP
Date: 2016–2023

Wilmar Headquarters

The design for Wilmar HQ provides laboratories and offices within a landscaped tropical garden setting. Located within Zaha Hadid Architects' One North masterplan, the site is an island block shared by One North Park, a linear park that permeates the entire area. Eric Parry Architects has led the design to RIBA Stage 3 with Singapore-based RSP Architects. This collaboration is to ensure the delivery of the design intent within the local regulatory framework, procurement and supply chain. The building is organic in form and is characterised by tiered landscape terraces that provide a garden aspect to each office level. The envelope is composed of ribbons of glass to provide 360° views, whilst 2m-deep horizontal ceramic fins provide solar shading to maximise the passive reduction of heat load and energy usage. At night, these glazed ceramic fins are illuminated. At ground level the building is lifted to allow a continuous landscape with the park, which is partially remodelled as a contemporary Chinese garden. An exhibition centre, auditorium and café animate this shaded space that is articulated by feature façades, composite tree-like structure and a sky oculus to provide a column of natural light.

C: Wilmar International Ltd
PM: Perennial Real Estate Holdings Limited
Local Architects and SE: RSP Architects Planners & Engineers (Pte) Ltd
M&E: Squire Mech Pte Ltd
QS: Threesixty Cost Management Pte. Ltd
LA: ICN Design International Pte Ltd
A: EP, JO, JT, LH, DL, CRD
Date: 2017–2021

Sir John Soane's Museum Exhibition

Open to the public from 20 February to 27 May 2019, this exhibition was entirely designed by Eric Parry Architects, bringing together a selection of Eric Parry's hand drawings and notebooks. The exhibits covered more than four decades of architectural observation, design and construction. Drawing notebooks were accommodated in bespoke display cabinets designed by Eric Parry Architects and placed amidst the permanent Museum Collection. Large hand drawings and sketches by Eric Parry were hung in the Galleries along with bespoke prints of the individual chapters of *Volumes 1, 2, 3* and *4* open to be consulted by the public. The exhibition included a short film commissioned and produced by Eric Parry Architects on the life of Eric Parry's drawing for 4 Pancras Square – from the drawing board, through construction, to the completed building. The office also contributed editorially and with contents to the book accompanying the exhibition, *Eric Parry: Drawing* (London: Sir John Soane's Museum, 2019), which contained an essay by David Leatherbarrow, and also a text by Owen Hopkins based on an interview with Eric Parry.

C: Sir John Soane's Museum
A: EP, JP*, EVP
Date: 2018–2019

St Martin-in-the-Fields II

The renewal project for St Martin-in-the-Fields, completed in 2008, was highly successful and created a masterplan framework to support congregational, cultural and commercial activities across the site. Over the last 12 years the scale and scope of the work of St Martin-in-the-Fields has exceeded original expectations and is placing strain on the existing and new fabric and facilities across the site. An initial feasibility and framework plan was completed by Eric Parry Architects in March 2019. This plan set out a 'visual sense of change' to support St Martin's continued growth. The feasibility and Stage 2 Report looked to establish a new series of overlays to the original masterplan that allows St Martin's and its buildings to reach out and support an ambitious, varied and flexibly programme of activities around theology, music, homelessness, public realm, sustainability and accessibility across St Martin's. Underpinning these ambitions is the need to maintain and repair the existing building fabric, continuing to improve the experience of the site for everyone who visits, and enabling St Martin's to expand and reach out beyond the traditional physical boundaries.

C: St Martin-in-the-Fields
A: EP, RK, CK, CB, AC
Date: 2018–2020

Clothworkers' Hall

The Clothworkers' Company commissioned EPA to develop proposals for the redevelopment of their site, where their new Livery Hall will be incorporated, and which achieved planning consent in April 2020. The current Clothworkers' sixth Hall was completed in 1958 following the near total destruction of the previous Hall during an air raid in 1941. The new Hall would be the seventh in a 490-year history on the site. The new Livery Hall consists of a four-storey pavilion building accessed from the north of the site off Fenchurch Street, and four basement levels which are home to the Client's function and ceremonial rooms. The scheme is structured around a sequence of spaces that form the ceremonial route from ground level, where one enters a glazed reception hall and descends through the foyer and reception spaces to the Livery Hall. A winter garden provides a focal point at the centre of the building, framing views back to the historic church tower of All Hallows Staining and inviting daylight to the public spaces around it.

C: The Clothworkers' Company
PM: Gardiner & Theobald
SE: ARUP
M&E: ARUP
QS: Alinea
A: EP, BD*, DL, SF*, AM, ALC, VG, RLL
Date: 2018-ongoing

Suvretta House Hotel

As early as 2008, Suvretta House recognised that it needed to take steps to redevelop itself in order to ensure its timeless appeal was in keeping with the wants and needs of its guests, resulting in their 2025 Vision. Eric Parry Architects was delighted to have worked on this vision with them. Now, as Suvretta House redevelop their Spa facilities, Eric Parry Architects anticipates the opportunity to work with the renowned establishment again. Our proposal for Suvretta House Hotel is articulated around the main building and weaves into the existing fabric, providing clarity of circulation. Each area is treated individually to allow its character to be defined along the journey through the hotel. Our proposed expansion to the southeast above the existing pool has been carefully tailored, giving consideration to scale, form and expression appropriate to its setting, and sympathetic to the main building. The integration of the proposal with the landscape has been a focus throughout the process. The landscape extends across the building, weaving in, around and through the levels, following the shape of the landscape.

C: AG Suvretta Haus
SE: Eckersley O'Callaghan
M&E: Skelly & Couch
A: EP, RK, LH, SF, RLL, VG, TJH, AO
Date: 2018–ongoing

The Goodsyard Plot 2

The client is a Joint Venture between Hammerson and Ballymore. Eric Parry Architects has been commissioned to develop a building for Plot 2 of The Bishopsgate Goodsyard masterplan to allow a detailed planning application to be submitted as part of an overall outline Planning Masterplan. It will include 15% affordable office space and 25–30% co-working spaces. (The affordable space may be part of the co-working space.) The building on Plot 2 is the flagship commercial building on the western prow of the Goodsyard delivering approximately 47,000 m² NIA office space and retail uses at ground and the Platform level, and is integrated into the heritage-rich, partly-listed world of brick archways, the remains of the Bishopsgate Goodsyard Station. The master planners are Faulkner Browns Architects. Eric Parry Architects' scheme has obtained Planning Permission in December 2020. EPA is currently working on the development of their Stage 2 information.

C: Ballymore and Hammerson (Joint Venture)
SE: WSP
M&E: Hoare Lea
QS: Gardiner & Theobald
A: EP, RK, TN, AH, CA, EVP, JS, ASM, EF, ELP, FW, SO, BT, SH, AKV
Date: 2018–ongoing

Project Mersey

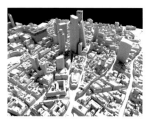

Project Mersey is for the redevelopment of Liverpool Street Station through the construction of a new 5-star Hyatt Andaz Hotel and 1 millionsqft of commercial office space. The Client is Sellar Property. The major stake holders are Network Rail, The Hyatt Hotel corporation and Transport for London. Consultation with these parties commenced in September 2018. The proposal is to introduce a second, street-level, concourse to the Network Rail station, freeing up more space for TfL at the lower concourse level. The construction of a new Andaz Hotel will free up the existing former Great Eastern Hotel (GEH) site for partial demolition or repurposing. The GEH is Grade II listed and has a number of significant interior spaces. The Hotel and Network Rail, TfL and Crossrail operations must be maintained throughout the construction process.

C: Sellar Property
A: EP, RK, PBA, JSC, RSW, FW
Date: 2018–ongoing

Chelsea Barracks Buildings 6 and 7 Interiors

Building 6 is to the west of the Chelsea Barracks development. The project involves the fit out of 48 apartments in varied arrangements, including duplex apartments at ground and lower ground floor. It also involves two penthouse apartments arranged over two floors. The northern penthouse apartment has been extended to provide an improved layout. and Building 7 is the third building in this phase, positioned to the south of the site addressing Chelsea Bridge Road. A marketing apartment within Building 7 will be fitted out along with the ground-floor entrance lobby, which is the main entrance to this phase of the development from Chelsea Bridge Road. The interior palette for the project was designed originally by 1508 in 2015/2016, and upgraded by Eric Parry Architects. The design includes many bespoke elements including joinery, stonework, wall panelling, architectural metalwork and bathroom furniture, therefore close coordination has been required throughout with specialist sub-contractors.

C: Qatari Diar
PM: Turner and Townsend
SE: Arup
M&E: Hoare Lea
QS: Gleeds
A: EP, RK, ARM, JSC, AC, CK, JH, VG, GC, CA, JWK, LVM, NA, OM, EVP
Date: 2019–ongoing

Capeners Close Residence

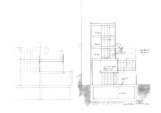

Creation of new art gallery and associated ancillary spaces, and new family residence on site of two existing mews properties. Capeners Close is a narrow, nineteenth-century mews with a courtyard, part of Westminster City Council's Belgravia Conservation Area. The proposal takes advantage of the reduction in the scale of the building from south to north by creating a cascading series of terraces which will be enlivened and screened with planting. The greening of the façades is a key component to grounding the new building in its place. Green planting on the terraces will add to the sense of a secret garden, whilst also maintaining the privacy of the neighbouring properties.

C: Private client
SE: Michael Hadi Associates
M&E: P3r Engineers
A: EP, DL, SF, TJH, LB
Date: 2018–ongoing

Ambassador's Residence Beijing

Following the Stage 2 Masterplan for the British Embassy Site in Beijing, China, the Foreign, Commonwealth & Development Office (FCDO) singled out the Ambassador's Residence as an opportunity to showcase a design that fully reflects Britain and its values, and sought an architect of the highest calibre to develop the concept and then work in collaboration with the overall project team during the delivery phase. The RIBA Competition was specifically held for the design of the Ambassador's Residence and Eric Parry Architects won the commission in late summer 2019. The Residence has a simple plan form that is nearly square with a central external court (the Court) which can be covered by a retractable glazed rooflight. The Residence is both private and public, accommodating the Ambassador's private apartment at the upper level, and the key representational rooms at ground level. The main representational rooms, the Reception and Dining room, have direct access to a landscaped garden that surrounds the house.

C: Foreign, Commonwealth & Development Office
PM: Atkins Global
SE: Atkins Global
M&E: Atkins Global
QS: Faithful Gould
A: EP, RK, SF, AM, RLL, TJH
Date: 2019–ongoing

The Fleet Street Estate

Eric Parry Architects was commissioned in 2019 to design and deliver a new, purpose-built 18-courtroom legal facility for Her Majesty's Courts and Tribunals Service (HMCTS) and a cutting-edge new headquarters building for the City of London Police at the heart of the historic Square Mile. The proposals for the buildings envisage a collection of distinct yet coherent designs. Materials have been carefully selected to respond to the location of each building within the masterplan and the wider area, as well as their specific functional requirements. Built to exemplar standards when it comes to accessibility and sustainability, the buildings are designed to last for a minimum of 125 years, and benefit from outstanding security and anti-terrorism credentials. At its heart, Salisbury Square will be enlarged and refocused as a gathering point for the development, a place people can enjoy. The square, dating back to the sixteenth century and currently presented as a hostile maneuvering space for motor vehicles, will see its civic identity restored. Designed with pedestrians and residents in mind, the new Salisbury Square will offer city workers a unique moment of stasis in a quarter of London characterised by restless movement.

C: City of London Corporation
PM: Avison Young
SE: Buro Happold
M&E and QS: Aecom
A: EP, LH*, TN, TS, GW, ASM, HT, ELP, LL, RSW, JSC, ZA, AKV, TB, AC, DG, CRD, SP, ARM, SB, LR, RC. AM, CK, SF, EVP, MCH, OM, TJH, EF, VG, BT, SO, MN, CD, AO, DMM, DPL, MMM
Date: 2019–ongoing

Seal House, City of London

Seal House is an office development next to the Fishmongers' Hall near London Bridge, where we were asked to replace a 1970s building (68,000 ft²). Our proposal allows for 213,000 ft² GIA over 11 stories, with the main body of the building (2nd–9th floors) consisting of a series of granite piers where the south and southeastern façades are load bearing. The building is supported by a series of massive painted steel prefabricated columns at 7.5- or 9-metre centres. There are restaurants both at ground and 11th-floor levels with views over the Thames and a publicly accessible terrace and garden can be accessed by two lifts from a lobby on The River Walk.

C: Middlecap
PM: Sellar Property / Turner and Townsend
SE and M&E: WSP
QS: Gardiner and Theobald
A: EP, PBA, NJ,FW, TJH, CK, AY, GN, JT
Date: 2019–ongoing

Kyobashi, Tokyo

Mixed-use tower in downtown Tokyo with retail, hotel and office facilities with a total floor area of 1,760,000 ft² including 35 above-ground levels and 4 basement levels, with a maximum height of 180 meters. The project will provide a key access node onto the space above the KK line, an elevated highway, which will be transformed into a 2km long green pedestrian space called the Tokyo Sky Corridor and will connect to Kyobashi Station to expand the wide-area underground pedestrian network. The project will contribute to urban renewal by developing urban infrastructure and introducing new urban functions that will contribute to the creation of a gateway to the international city of Tokyo with a high level of pedestrian circulation. Construction is scheduled to begin in 2025 and be completed in 2029.

C: Kyobashi 3-chome East Area Redevelopment Preparatory Association
PM: Tokyo Tatemono Co., Ltd
Local Architect: Nihon Sekkei, Inc.
SE: Nihon Sekkei, Inc.
M&E: Nihon Sekkei, Inc.
A: EP, JO, AM, AK, PBA, RLL
Date: 2019–ongoing

Staff List

The order of initials reflects design responsibility, * marks project team leader. Where this was passed on between designs (1) and construction (2) the * is followed by the respective figure.

References for Design Team:

C   Client
PM   Project Manager
SE   Structural Engineer
M&E Mechanical Engineering
       Consultants
QS   Quantity Surveyor
LA   Landscape Architect
A   EPA Team

EP   Eric Parry
BA Hons (Newcastle), MA (Cantab), MA (RCA), AADipl, Hon DA (Bath), RIBA, RA
founded the practice in 1983

LH   Lee Higson
BA Hons (Leeds), DipArch (London Met), RIBA
worked at EPA from 2006 to the present
appointed associate in 2007
appointed associate director in 2010
appointed director in 2018

NJ   Nick Jackson
BA Hons (Cantab), MA (Cantab), DipArch (Cantab), RIBA
worked at EPA from 1990 to 2018
appointed director in 1997

JS   Justin Sayer
BA (Oxon), BSc (East London), DipArch (UCL, DBA), RIBA
worked at EPA from 1996 to the present
appointed associate in 2003
appointed associate director in 2007

SF   Sofia Ferreira
BA (Hons), DipArch, ARB
worked at EPA from 2006 to the present
appointed associate in 2017
appointed associate director in 2023

MC   Merit Claussen
Textile designer, Architect RIBA
worked at EPA from 1999 to 2016
appointed associate in 2007
appointed associate director in 2010

RC   Ros Cohen
BA Hons (Cantab), MA (Cantab), DipArch (UEL), Architect ARB
worked at EPA from 1998 to 2001 and 2003 to the present
appointed associate in 2010

RSW   Rupert Willard
BSc Hons (UCL), DipArch (LSBU), ARB
worked at EPA from 2015 to the present
appointed associate in 2020

LB   Lewis Benmore
BA (Hons), DipArch, MArch, RHS Cert, ARB
worked at EPA from 2008 to the present
appointed associate in 2023

CB   Christopher Burton
MA Hons (Mackintosh), DipArch (Mackintosh), ARB
worked at EPA from 2004 to 2020
appointed associate in 2010

RK   Robert Kennett
MA (Cantab), DipArch (Cantab), RIBA
worked at EPA from 1989 to the present
appointed director in 1997

JG   Jin Georgiou
MENG (ChemE), ACGI
worked at EPA from 2006 to the present
appointed director in 2020

TP   Tanya Parkin
BSc Hons (QUB), DipArch DipBRS (OBU), RIBA
worked at EPA from 2001 to 2021
appointed associate in 2006
appointed associate director in 2016
appointed director in 2018

TN   Takayuki Nakajima
Arch (IJBA, CPAIJ)
worked at EPA from 2013 to the present
appointed associate in 2017
appointed associate director in 2019

ASM Asher Meltzer
B.Arch, ARB
worked at EPA from 2014 to the present
appointed associate in 2020
appointed associate director in 2023

TL   Tim Lynch
BA Hons (Newcastle), DipArch (Mackintosh), RIBA
worked at EPA from 2004 to 2017
appointed associate in 2007
appointed associate director in 2010

ARM Anil Mistry
BA (Hons), DipArch, MArch, ARB
worked at EPA from 2006 to the present
appointed associate in 2014

AM   Aya Maeda
AADipl, ARB
worked at EPA from 2005 to the present
appointed associate in 2022

TS   Tom Sweet
worked at EPA from 2013 to the present
appointed associate in 2020

DL   Damien Lee
BSc Hons, DipArch, ARB
worked at EPA from 2006 to 2020
appointed associate in 2014

JO   Julian Ogiwara
BA Hons (UEL), DipArch (UEL), RIBA
worked at EPA from 2000 to the present
appointed associate in 2007
appointed director in 2010

RD   Robert Dawson
BA Hons (Birmingham), DipArch (Oxford Brookes), ARB
worked at EPA from 2006 to the present
appointed associate in 2010
appointed associate director in 2016
appointed director in 2023

PBA Paul Barke-Asuni
BArch, MA (Princeton), ARB
worked at EPA from 2011 to the present
appointed associate in 2014
appointed associate director in 2020

SH   Sven Heimann
Dipl.-Ing., MArch, ARB
worked at EPA from 2014 to the present
appointed associate in 2017

CK   Catharin Knuth
Dipl.-Ing, MA
worked at EPA from 2008 to the present
appointed associate in 2022

MN   Markus Nurkkala
BA (Hons), DipArch, ARB
worked at EPA from 2014 to the present
appointed associate in 2020

CT   Claudia Tschunko
Dipl.-Ing. Arch. (Stuttgart), Architect ARB
worked at EPA from 2007 to 2018
appointed associate in 2010

BD   Brendan Durkin
BA Hons (Kingston), DipArch (London Metropolitan), ARB
worked at EPA from 2006 to the present
appointed associate in 2014
appointed associate director in 2019
appointed director in 2023

JSC Jonathan Schöning
BA, DipArch (Mackintosh), Architect ARB
worked at EPA from 2011 to the present
appointed associate in 2017

AG   Aura Gnerucci
MArch, ARB
worked at EPA from 2016 to the present
appointed associate in 2023

HT   Hannah Tourell
BA (Hons), DipArch, ARB
worked at EPA from 2015 to the present
appointed associate in 2023

GGP Guy Parkinson
BA (Hons), DipArch, ARB
worked at EPA from 2007 to 2018
appointed associate in 2014

GW   Gary Watkin
BSc, PGDip, DPS, ARB
worked at EPA from 2014 to the present
appointed associate in 2019

ELP Emily Posey
BSc Hons (Bath), MArch (Westminster), ARB
worked at EPA from 2014 to the present
appointed associate in 2023

MM Mike Mc Mahon
BSc Arch (Hons), DipArch, MArch, ARB
worked at EPA from 2013 to 2022
appointed associate in 2019

Architectural

AA	Abbas Afsar
AC	Abigail Connor
AG	Aura Gnerucci
AH	Alison Ho
AK	Akira Kindo
AKV	Aneliya Kavrakova
ALC	Alessandra Camiz
AM	Aya Maeda
ANM	Aesha Mehta
AO	Andrius Ovsiukas
ARM	Anil Mistry
ASM	Asher Meltzer
AW	Alexander Watt
AY	Alfred Yeung
AZH	Ahmadzia Hasas
BD	Brendan Durkin
BF	Brian Fitzgerald
BL	Brenda Leonard
BT	Benedek Takács
CA	Charlotte Airey
CB	Christopher Burton
CD	Christopher Drummond
CJ	Chris Jones
CK	Catharin Knuth
CL	Carl Laffan
CLK	Cecilie Kjeldsen
CRD	Charles Debelle
CSL	Chloe Spiby-Loh
CT	Claudia Tschunko
DC	Damien Clayton
DG	Derek Gibbons
DK	Dan Kimber
DL	Damien Lee
DMM	Dónal Mc Mullan
DP	David Pérez
DPL	Daniel Linham
EA	Eduardo Argüelles
EC	Elena Cavagnera
ED	Edward Dyhouse
EF	Eliot Foy
EGP	Eugenia Pavone
EH	Eimear Hanratty
EK	Edd Kilvert
EKL	Ethan Liu
ELP	Emily Posey
EM	Edel McGee
EP	Eric Parry
EVP	Eva Pospechova

FW	Fei Wu
GB	Gianni Barberi
GC	Giuseppina Cacciapuoti
GGP	Guy Parkinson
GN	Gregory Niedzwiecki
GW	Gary Watkin
HS	Harry Stueli
HT	Hannah Tourell
IS	Iulia Statica
JB	Jordan Burton
JF	Jamie Flynn
JFR	Jeremy Foster
JFS	Jian See
JH	Joshua Hinh
JIS	Jiehwoo Seung
JK	Jamie Kuehn
JM	James McNeill
JO	Julian Ogiwara
JP	José de Paiva
JS	Justin Sayer
JSC	Jonathan Schöning
JT	Jessica Tettelaar
JWK	Jae Whan Kim
KB	Kenet Bakamovic
KP	Katharina Parsons
KS	Krystin Schwendel Smith
LB	Lewis Benmore
LG	Louise Godfrey
LH	Lee Higson
LL	Luísa Lopes
LM	Lee McKinley
LMB	Lisa Basu
LR	Lara Raposo da Silva
LVM	Llewellyn Vardon McLeod
LW	Lu Wang
MC	Merit Claussen
MCH	Myles Chapman
MH	Max Hubbard
MIP	Melissa Patterson
MJ	Michelle Jeremiah
MM	Mike Mc Mahon
MMM	Molly Mummery
MN	Markus Nurkkala
MP	Michael Perkins
MV	Michael Vale
MWM	Milliam Mbugua
NA	Nazeer Alnazal
NG	Nikolina Georgieva

NJ	Nick Jackson
OM	Omar Manshi
PBA	Paul Barke-Asuni
PF	Paul Fielding
RC	Ros Cohen
RD	Robert Dawson
RK	Robert Kennett
RL	Rebecca Lim
RLL	Roo Lam Lau
RP	Richard Prest
RRP	Ruby Penny
RSW	Rupert Willard
RWC	Russell Clayton
SB	Sophia Bannert
SF	Sofia Ferreira
SH	Sven Heimann
SO	Sarah Oxley
SP	Sara del Piñal
TA	Thomas Atkinson
TB	Thomas Blain
TJH	T J Hartnett
TL	Tim Lynch
TN	Takayuki Nakajima
TP	Tanya Parkin
TS	Tom Sweet
VG	Valentina Grittini
VL	Victoria Leyland
WA	William Aitken
WW	William Wang
XL	Xiaowei Liang
YH	Yu Hin Chun
ZA	Zoe Arnold
ZP	Zoe Panayi

Non-architectural

Becky Atkinson
Craig Lochhead
Duncan Macdonald
Emma Shaw
Huda Patel
Jesse Oppong
Jessica O'Connor Tomlin
Jin Georgiou
Joanne Gold
Katherine da Silva
Kesh Wang
Linnee Wen
Mandii Pope
Oluwatobi Akinde
Robert Hood
Roma McCook
Russell Watson
Theresa Badero
Winnie Delissen

Photo Credits

Cover: DL

4.	DBOX
12.	GS
14.	DL
17.	DMW
19.	DL
20.	The Museum of Modern Art, New York/Scala, Florence
23.	DL

Fen Court

26.	JH
30.	DL
31.	DL
33.	DL
34.	GS
35.	DL
36.	DL
38.	DL
39.	DL

30 St James's Square

40.	DL
42.	EPA
43.	EPA (left)
43.	DL (right)
46.	EPA
47.	EPA
48.	DL
49.	DL (left)
49.	EPA (right)
52.	DL
53.	DL

Carlton House Terrace

54.	DL
56.	DL
58.	DL
60.	DL
61.	DL
63.	DL
65.	DL

London Residence

66.	DL
69.	DL
70.	DL
71.	DL
74.	EPA
75.	DL
76.	DL
77.	DL
78.	DL
79.	DL

One Chamberlain Square

80.	DL
82.	Library of Birmingham
87.	GS (left)
87.	DL (right)
88.	DL
90.	DL
91.	DL
92.	EPA
94.	GS (left)
94.	DMW (right)
95.	DL

Wilmar Headquarters

96.	FO
98.	EPA
99.	FO
102.	FO
103.	FO
105.	FO
106.	EPA
107.	EPA
108.	FO
109.	FO

Vicarage Gate House

110.	DL
112.	DL
113.	DL
114.	DL
117.	DL
118.	DL
119.	DL
120.	DL
121.	DL

111 Buckingham Palace Road

122.	DL
126.	DL
127.	DL
129.	DL
130.	DL
131.	DL

Sir John Soane's Museum Exhibition

132.	DL
135.	DL
136.	DL
138.	DL
139.	DL
140.	DL
141.	DL
142.	DL
143.	DL

Lipton Residence II

144.	JH
147.	JH
149.	JH
150.	JH
151.	JH
152.	JH
153.	JH
154.	JH
156.	JH

Cambridge University Press & Assessment

158.	DL
166.	DL
167.	DL
168.	DL
169.	DL
170.	DL
171.	DL

Chelsea Barracks

172.	DL
177.	DL (above)
177.	EP (below)
180.	V1
183.	DBOX
184.	DL
185.	DL
186.	DL (left)
186.	GS (right)
187.	DL
188.	DL
189.	EP
191.	DL
192.	DL

1 Undershaft

194.	DBOX
197.	EPA
201.	DBOX
202.	DBOX
205.	AP
206.	DBOX

Photographers

AP	Andrew Putler
DL	Dirk Lindner
DMW	Dagmar Motycka Weston
EP	Eric Parry
EPA	Eric Parry Architects
FO	Fabian Ong
GS	Grant Smith
JH	James Harris

Visualisations

DBOX	
V1	Visualisation One

Acknowledgements

Our profound thanks are due to Dagmar Motycka Weston for the care and balance she has achieved in both her introductory essay and texts that describe so interestingly the context, ambitions and outcome of the broad range of scales of making that are represented in this volume. Together we visited all the projects with the exception of the Headquarters for Wilmar in Singapore, where distance and COVID restrictions meant that a virtual tour of the site and the building had to suffice. Dagmar was particularly diligent in her further questioning of those involved in each of the projects in order to be sure of the interpretations she made.

We were also particularly delighted that David Leatherbarrow accepted the invitation to write an introductory essay, not least because whilst our journeys have diverged widely, we have common roots in the academic 'hot house' that existed in London in the late 1970s. His essay opens a door to a distinct and erudite school of architectural thought and practice that has become perhaps the most important voice of its kind today.

To draw all the material into a coherent whole has been the testing task of José de Paiva and we know that it would have been unrequited but for his clarity of purpose, dignified self-depreciation and steely determination. The majority of the line drawings have been prepared for publication by our practice in dialogue with members of the respective project teams. Daniel Benneworth-Gray has once again been responsible for the graphic design and layout of the volume and we are very grateful for his continuing contribution.

We would like to thank Anna Danby from Artifice for the unreserved support she and her team have given us in reaching the point of publication. Artifice has been an essential part of our reflective journey – bravo!

Colophon

© 2023 SJH Group, Eric Parry Architects, the photographers and authors

This book is published by Artifice Press Limited, a company registered in England and Wales with company number 11182108. Artifice Press is an imprint within the SJH Group. Copyright is owned by the SJH Group Limited. All rights reserved.

Artifice Press
The Maple Building
39–51 Highgate Road
London NW5 1RT
United Kingdom

+44 (0)20 8371 4047
office@artificeonline.com
www.artificeonline.com

Design by Daniel Benneworth-Gray for
Eric Parry Architects
danielgray.com

Printed in Italy by Faenza Printing Industries S.p.A

ISBN: 978 1 911339 53 3

British Library Cataloguing in Publication data:
A CIP record for this book is available from the British Library.

Neither this publication nor any part of it may be reproduced, stored in a retrieval system or transmitted in any form or by any means, electronic, mechanical, photocopying, recording or otherwise, without the prior permission of the SJH Group or the appropriately accredited copyright holder.

All information in this publication is verified to the best of the author's and publisher's ability. However, Artifice Press and the SJH Group do not accept responsibility for any loss arising from reliance on it. Where opinion is expressed, it is that of the author and does not necessarily coincide with the editorial views of the publisher. The publishers have made all reasonable efforts to trace the copyright owners of the images reproduced herein, and to provide an appropriate acknowledgement in the book.

Also available:

Eric Parry Architects Volume 1
ISBN 978 1 906155 62 9

Eric Parry Architects Volume 2
ISBN 978 1 906155 25 4

Eric Parry Architects Volume 1 & 2 Box Set
ISBN 978 1 906155 63 6

Eric Parry Architects Volume 3
ISBN 978 1 908967 03 9

Eric Parry Architects Volume 4
ISBN 978 1 91133931 1

Eric Parry Architects Volume 3 & 4 Box Set
ISBN 978 1 911339 32 8